The OECD Guidelines for Multinational Enterprises

The OECD Guidelines for Multinational Enterprises

Peter Tergeist

This book was originally published as a monograph in the International Encyclopaedia of Laws/Labour Law and Industrial Relations.

General Editors: Roger Blanpain, Frank Hendrickx

Wolters Kluwer

Published by:
Kluwer Law International B.V.
PO Box 316
2400 AH Alphen aan den Rijn
The Netherlands
Website: www.wklawbusiness.com

Sold and distributed in North, Central and South America by:
Wolters Kluwer Legal & Regulatory U.S.
7201 McKinney Circle
Frederick, MD 21704
United States of America
Email: customer.service@wolterskluwer.com

Sold and distributed in all other countries by:
Turpin Distribution Services Ltd.
Stratton Business Park
Pegasus Drive, Biggleswade
Bedfordshire SG18 8TQ
United Kingdom
Email: kluwerlaw@turpin-distribution.com

Printed on acid-free paper

ISBN 978-90-411-6951-8

e-Book: ISBN 978-90-411-6967-9
web-PDF: ISBN 978-90-411-6990-7

This title is available on www.kluwerlawonline.com

Printed and Bound by CPI Group (UK) Ltd, Croydon, CR0 4YY.

FSC
MIX
FSC® C103993

The Author

Dr Peter Tergeist worked as an analyst in the Directorate for Employment, Labour and Social Affairs of the Organization for Economic Co-operation and Development (OECD) between the late 1980s and his retirement in 2011. He holds an MA degree in Political Science from the University of Pennsylvania and a Dr rer. pol. degree from the Free University of Berlin. Before joining the OECD, he worked as a social researcher at the Wissenschaftszentrum (Science Centre) Berlin.

Following a period in the 1980s and 1990s as Secretary to the OECD Working Party on Industrial Relations, he has worked on a range of labour market policy, vocational training and labour relations issues. He is the author and editor of a number of articles and books on labour market and labour relations topics, and has been contributing numerous chapters to the annual OECD Employment Outlook.

The author has made use of a limited amount of text originating from the monograph on the OECD Guidelines dated January 1985, written by Professor Roger Blanpain

The Author

Table of Contents

Table of Contents

List of Abbreviations

BIAC	Business and Industry Advisory Committee to the OECD
CGT	*Confédération générale du travail*
ETUC	European Trade Union Confederation
EU	European Union
ILO	International Labour Organization
CIME	Committee on International Investment and Multinational Enterprises
INV	Investment Committee
ITUC	International Trade Union Confederation
MNEs	Multinational Enterprises
NCP	National Contact Point
NGO	Non-governmental organization
OECD	Organization for Economic Co-operation and Development
OEEC	Organization for European Economic Co-operation
TUAC	Trade Union Advisory Committee to the OECD
UN	United Nations
WTO	World Trade Organisation

List of Abbreviations

1–3

Introduction

1. Corporate social responsibility has become an issue of growing importance over the past few decades, accompanying the rapid evolution of global business. A multiplicity of actors and standard-setting initiatives operate in the area. First, there are thousands of company codes of conduct, specifying responsibilities and commitments in environmental standards, employee relations, disclosure practices, and other areas. Many consumers, as well, seem ready to base their purchase decisions, at least in part, on perception of a company's social reputation and ethical behaviour. Next, codes of conduct, guidelines, or declarations of principles governing the behaviour of enterprises – in particular multinationals – have also been drawn up by international organizations, such as the UN, ILO, OECD and the EU.

2. The OECD was first to promulgate its Guidelines for Multinational Enterprises, in June 1976 – guidelines which were substantially revised on several occasions, in particular in 2000 and 2011. The ILO followed suit with its Tripartite Declaration of Principles concerning Multinational Enterprises and Social Policy in November 1977 – the latest revision dating from 2006. Another code of conduct promulgated at the level of inter-governmental organizations is the UN Global Compact, initiated in 1999 by UN Secretary-General Kofi Annan. Of relevance in this context are also, *inter alia*, the ILO Declaration on Fundamental Principles and Rights at Work, the UN Declaration on Human Rights, the Guiding Principles on Business and Human Rights of the UN Human Rights Council, and the OECD Corporate Governance principles. Among other, private sector, global instruments for corporate responsibility are the Social Accountability 8000 standard, and the Global Reporting Initiative (GRI).

3. The OECD Guidelines for Multinational Enterprises were formulated in 1976 as one of several elements of an OECD Council Declaration on International Investment and Multinational Enterprises. They are recommendations to enterprises from OECD and other adhering governments to help ensure that multinational businesses conform to advanced international standards in a number of areas and adjust to the traditions and policies of their host countries. Thus, they are meant to strengthen mutual confidence between enterprises and the societies in which they operate and to enhance the contribution to equitable growth and social progress made by multinational enterprises (MNEs). These voluntary standards cover not only labour and employment relations, but deal with a range of issues relating to corporate conduct, such as observation of human rights, information disclosure, environmental protection, bribery, competition and consumer protection. The 1976 text and its numerous updates since then are also a response to many reports of poor working conditions, abusive wage practices and violations of core labour standards, such as the use of child labour. While in the past, these problems applied mainly to MNEs headquartered in developed countries, they increasingly refer also to practices by MNEs from emerging economies.

4. In the text that follows, we focus our attention on the OECD Guidelines' content and the accompanying inter-governmental consultation and implementation procedures, in their revised version as of 2011. Chapter 1 gives a short description of the institutional framework in which the Guidelines were negotiated and are currently operating, namely of the OECD itself, its Investment Committee (INV, previously CIME), the advisory bodies of business and labour (BIAC and TUAC) and OECD Watch representing NGOs. Chapter 2 includes a general examination of the Guidelines text (their genesis and main content) and presents an overview of complaint cases between 1976 and today, while Chapter 3 examines some broader issues such as the Guidelines' voluntary character, supply-chain management and responsible business conduct in weak governance zones.

5. Chapter 4 focuses in more detail on the labour relations content of the Guidelines. In that chapter we examine the detailed provisions of the Guidelines recommendations on Employment and Industrial Relations, in the light of clarifications issued by the Investment Committee between 1976 and 1999, the work subsequently undertaken by the National Contact Points (NCPs), and the official commentary agreed by the signatory countries in 2000 and 2011. Chapter 5 discusses issues concerning the implementation of the Guidelines, above all the conciliation and mediation of NCPs in complaint cases ('specific instances'). This is followed by the bibliography and index. The full texts of the OECD Declaration on International Investment and Multinational Enterprises, the OECD Guidelines on Multinational Enterprises (main text and commentary), and the OECD Council Decision and Procedural Guidance on implementation matters can be found in the Codex of this *Encyclopaedia* under Regional Instruments/OECD.

Chapter 1. The Institutional Framework

§1. The Organization for Economic Co-operation and Development (OECD)

6. The OECD's basic structure and functions are outlined in more detail in Volume 2 of this *Encyclopaedia.*[1] The organization was set up in 1961 under a Convention signed in Paris on 14 December 1960, which lists the OECD's basic aims as contributing to economic development and trade expansion in the world economy, and achieving sustainable economic growth and employment as well as a rising standard of living in member countries. There are currently (as of mid 2016) 35 members of the organization: Australia, Austria, Belgium, Canada, Chili, the Czech Republic, Denmark, Estonia, Finland, France, Germany, Greece, Hungary, Iceland, Ireland, Israel, Italy, Japan, Korea, Latvia, Luxembourg, Mexico, the Netherlands, New Zealand, Norway, Poland, Portugal, Slovakia, Slovenia, Spain, Sweden, Switzerland, Turkey, the United Kingdom and the United States. In mid 2016, candidates for accession were Colombia, Lithuania and Costa Rica, while membership negotiations with the Russian Federation which had been ongoing since 2007, were suspended in 2014. The Commission of the European Union also takes part in the OECD's work, in accordance with a special Protocol to the OECD Convention, while the special membership status of Yugoslavia, which was revoked in the early 1990s, is now only of historical interest.

7. The principal political organs of the OECD are the Council, which consists of representatives of all Member States and usually meets once a year at ministerial level, and the Executive Committee, elected annually by the Council, which approves the annual programme of work and budget for the Committees. The Secretariat is led by a Secretary-General, currently (2016) Angel Gurria, a former cabinet minister from Mexico, who was designated in 2006 and is now in his third term.

8. The Council has established over 30 committees attended by member country delegates, as well as over 100 subsidiary working parties and expert groups that guide the work of the Secretariat and serve to facilitate the exchange of views and coordination of policies among countries within their fields of expertise. One of these is the Investment Committee (INV), created by the Council in 2004, the successor body to the Committee on International Investment and Multinational Enterprises (CIME), established in 1975. It was this latter Committee which was charged in 1976 with overseeing the OECD Guidelines for Multinational Enterprises.

9. Only governments are members of the OECD, unlike the ILO for example, which is tripartite and composed equally of governments, employers' and trade union organizations. However, business and trade union organizations have been

1. Peter Tergeist *et al.*, *The Organization for Economic Co-operation and Development, International Encyclopaedia for Labour Law and Industrial Relations*, Vol. 2, supplement 235, October 2000.

granted consultative status and regularly participate in the work of committees and working parties (see the sections on BIAC and TUAC below). Over the past decade, NGOs have also been increasingly active in discussing and monitoring OECD work, notably at the Investment Committee.

§2. The Investment Committee (INV)

10. The OECD Directorate for Financial and Enterprise Affairs services several committees composed of country delegates, among which are the Investment Committee (INV), the Committee on Financial Markets and the Corporate Governance Committee. The INV Committee, in particular, is responsible for the OECD instruments in the field of international investment, by developing policies towards international capital movements, direct investment and MNEs, and by interpreting and overseeing the implementation of the 1976/2011 Declaration on International Investment and Multinational Enterprises. Among other legal instruments in international investment, the INV Committee also handles the Code of Liberalization of Capital Movements, the Code of Liberalization of Current Invisible Operations (covering cross-border services), and the Convention on Combating Bribery of Foreign Officials in International Business Transactions.

11. CIME, the INV Committee's predecessor body, was set up in January 1975, particularly in order to negotiate and draft the initial set of guidelines for MNEs and provide intergovernmental consultation procedures. After the adoption of the OECD Guidelines, the committee was given the responsibility of regularly reviewing their relevance and implementation, of issuing 'clarifications' in response to requests on specific or general Guidelines provisions, and organizing appropriate promotional activities. Under its current (2013–2018) mandate, the Committee – reorganized and renamed INV in 2004 – is charged with, *inter alia:*

- maintaining and expanding transparent policy frameworks for investment, capital movements and services;
- serving as a policy forum on best practices related to international investment and MNEs;
- promoting dialogue with relevant international organizations, the business community, labour unions and NGOs;
- overseeing the OECD MNE Guidelines, in particular, holding exchanges of views on matters covered by them, hearing reports from so-called 'national contact points' (NCPs) on complaint cases ('specific instances') and implementation issues, and giving interpretations and clarifications of certain Guidelines provisions, when necessary.[2]

2. See the Terms of reference of the Committee as decided by the OECD Council, http://webnet3.oecd.org/OECDgroups/; the May 2011 Council Decision on Implementation Procedures; as well as further discussion in Chapter 5 of this monograph.

12. The INV Committee is composed of representatives of the 35 OECD member governments, while the 11 additional countries (in mid 2016) that adhere to the Declaration (Argentina, Brazil, Colombia, Costa Rica, Egypt, Jordan, Lithuania, Morocco, Peru, Romania and Tunisia) are able to attend its sessions dealing with the instrument. Most of them are civil servants representing the competent national ministries, i.e. mainly the ministries of economic affairs, industry, trade, foreign affairs, or finance. Some international organizations can participate as observers (World Bank, IMF, UNCTAD and WTO). The OECD Secretariat normally takes part in Committee meetings with a small number of staff and provides input with various types of documents and background analyses. Remarkably, ministries of labour have not been much involved in the past, although a majority of cases and issues relating to the OECD Guidelines, which were discussed in the Investment Committee after 1976, have related to labour and industrial relations problems. Since 2000, after the strengthening of implementation procedures via National Contact Points (NCPs), labour ministries tend to be more involved since, in many countries, their representatives form part of the NCPs.

13. A large number of country delegates attend the periodic Committee meetings. About 60 to 80 persons are usually listed as delegates, mainly from the 34 OECD member countries, but also the EU Commission and additional countries adhering to the Guidelines. During discussions about Guidelines updates, as in 2010/11, their number can easily reach over 100.

14. Several working parties (or working groups) operate under the INV: *inter alia*, the Working Group on International Investment Statistics; and the Advisory Group on Investment and Development. Another Working Party is charged with assisting the Investment Committee in implementing the Declaration on International Investment and Multinational Enterprises, in particular with respect to the Guidelines on Multinational Enterprises. This Working Party, first created in 1977, has changed names several times (in the early 2000s it changed from Working Party on the OECD Guidelines to Working Party of the Investment Committee). It traditionally meets 'back-to-back' with the committee, usually three to four times a year, and many of its delegates are also members of the INV.

15. In 2012, the Working Party of the Investment Committee was split up into one Working Party dealing exclusively with the OECD Guidelines, and another dealing with the other elements of the Declaration on International Investment and Multinational Enterprises (see paragraph 38 below) and further OECD instruments in the field of international investment policies. The former Working Party was named Working Party for Responsible Business Conduct (WPRBC)

16. The Working Party for Responsible Business Conduct is operating (up to 2018) under the following mandate:

1. The Working Party … shall assist the Investment Committee in implementing section I of the Declaration on International Investment and Multinational Enterprises with respect to its responsibilities in relation to the OECD

Guidelines for Multinational Enterprises (hereafter the Guidelines) and related Decision.

2. The Working Party shall carry out the following tasks:

   (i) To assist in enhancing the effectiveness of the Guidelines and fostering the functional equivalence of National Contact Points;
   (ii) To assist, in co-operation with the National Contact Points, in the implementation of the 'proactive agenda';
   (iii) To engage, on behalf of the Investment Committee, with non-adhering countries on matters covered by the Guidelines, in particular with those non-adhering countries that have a special interest in promoting the principles and standards in the Guidelines …

17. The Mandate also notes that the Working Party shall consult, as appropriate, other OECD bodies, international organizations or experts, as well as BIAC, TUAC and the NGO clearing-house, OECD Watch; and that non-Members adhering to the OECD Guidelines are invited to participate in the work of the Working Party relating to this instrument.

18. The Working Party (under its different titles) and the full committee have been cooperating in the periodic reviews of the Guidelines which were mandated by the 1976 Council Declaration. Reviews were held in 1979, 1982, 1984, 1991, 1999/2000, and most recently in 2010/11. The initial reviews resulted in some minor changes in the Guidelines text, when provisions were changed or added based on the experience and insights gained during complaints and clarification procedures. In 1991, a full new chapter on the environment was added. The 1999/2000 review led to a complete overhaul and to the addition of several new chapters as well as a long set of commentaries, parts of which were taken from previous clarifications by the CIME.

19. The financial crisis that struck in 2008 hastened the need for an additional review, and in 2009 OECD governments asked the INV Committee for an update of the Guidelines that would 'enhance their relevance and clarify the responsibilities of the private sector'. Accompanying its adoption of a revised Guidelines text, the 2011 OECD Council Decision requested periodic reviews and updating of the Guidelines instrument and asked the INV Committee to report to the Council on matters covered by the Guidelines, where it 'shall take account of reports by National Contact Points, the views expressed by the advisory bodies, OECD Watch, other international partners and non-adhering countries as appropriate'.

§3. The Role of Advisory Bodies

20. The May 2011 Decision by the OECD Council on Implementation Procedures of the OECD Guidelines for Multinational Enterprises lays down that the INV Committee:

shall periodically invite the Business and Industry Advisory Committee to the OECD (BIAC) and the Trade Union Advisory Committee to the OECD (TUAC) (the 'advisory bodies'), OECD Watch, as well as other international partners to express their views on matters covered by the Guidelines. In addition, exchanges of views with the advisory bodies on these matters may be held at their request.

Furthermore, in its reports to the Council, the Committee 'shall take account of … the views expressed by the advisory bodies'. Similar provisions were already contained in the original 1976 Council Decision.

21. In fact, the OECD's advisory committees representing both labour and the business community have been influential partners both in the design and the implementation of the Guidelines from the outset. Most of the requests for clarification of individual Guidelines provisions which were submitted to the CIME between 1976 and 2000, were raised by TUAC which argued at length against specific company conduct in violation of Guidelines provisions (after which BIAC would tend to defend the company in question and argue against any text consisting of criticizing individual enterprises). More recently, of about 330 complaints raised with National Contact Points between 2000 and 2015 (according to the OECD database of specific instances), a majority has dealt with the chapter on Employment and Industrial Relations and a little less than half were submitted by trade union members of TUAC.[3]

22. Extensive discussions with the social partner organizations were again held in the run-up to the 2000 and 2011 Guidelines reviews, each time with a large number of consultative sessions between them and both the Investment Committee and its Working Party, and a number of position papers provided by both BIAC and TUAC. Starting in 2000, the Guidelines negotiations gave rise to a new phenomenon for the OECD, insofar as many of these consultative sessions also contained input from other non-governmental organizations (such as Friends of the Earth, Oxfam or the World Wildlife Fund), although these groups did not enjoy the long-established standing of BIAC and TUAC as the OECD's official advisory groups.

23. A number of NGOs, in total over 80 civil society organizations working on human rights, labour rights, consumer rights, transparency, environment and sustainable development, subsequently joined forces and in 2003 formed a clearing-house called OECD Watch to help facilitate NGO activities around the OECD Guidelines and the work of the Investment Committee. During the negotiations for the 2011 update, OECD Watch participated in the discussions on an equal footing with the established advisory committees. Together with BIAC and TUAC, OECD Watch is now considered an 'accredited stakeholder'.[4]

3. Only four cases in total were submitted by business.
4. OECD Watch's self-characterization is that of 'an international network of civil society organizations promoting corporate accountability. The purpose of OECD Watch is to inform the wider NGO

I. BIAC

24. The Business and Industry Advisory Committee (BIAC) was constituted in March 1962, as an independent organization officially recognized by the OECD as being representative of business and industry.[5] BIAC's role is mainly to provide the OECD Secretariat with policy advice reflecting the business point of view; ensuring that business needs are as much as possible addressed in OECD policy instruments; and providing members with timely information on OECD policies and their implications for business and industry. This is being done through annual consultations with the OECD Committee for Liaison with Non-governmental Organizations, through meetings with representatives of various OECD committees, and substantive work in BIAC policy groups. The organization has noted repeatedly that it considers responsible business conduct as promoted by the OECD's MNE Guidelines 'an essential part of an open investment climate and in the best interest of business'.

25. BIAC's membership consists of over 40 business and industry organizations from the 34 OECD member countries, business organizations with observer status from 13 observer countries (from Argentina to South Africa) and several dozen Associate Experts, i.e. sectoral supra-national business organizations.

26. The BIAC Secretariat, consisting of the Secretary-General and a small staff, is located in Paris near OECD headquarters. Its chief functions are to maintain close contact with the OECD Secretariat, keep members informed of internal OECD policy developments and to organize and coordinate the activities of BIAC's committees and working groups.

27. BIAC's General Assembly, comprising the heads and other representatives of its member federations, normally meets in full session once a year to set general priorities and approve the BIAC work programme and budget.

28. The Executive Board is the executive arm of the General Assembly, and is charged with overseeing policy implementation. Its current Chairman (as of 2016) is Phil O'Reilly, Chief Executive of BusinessNZ, New Zealand's largest business advocacy group.

29. BIAC's over 30 policy groups, drawn from member organizations and private industry, cover the major aspects of OECD work most relevant to business, with the object of formulating common viewpoints and policy priorities. Because of the nature of its relationship with the OECD, BIAC's range of activities naturally corresponds broadly to that of the OECD itself. Areas covered by the policy groups

---

community about policies and activities of the OECD's Investment Committee and to test the effectiveness of the OECD Guidelines for Multinational Enterprises' (http://oecdwatch.org/). According to the organization's newsletter, it submitted even more complaints than TUAC (*OECD Watch*, Quarterly Case Update, Vol. 10, Iss. 1, June 2015).

5. See BIAC annual report of activities, and BIAC website www.biac.org and www.biac.org/MNE_Guidelines.htm.

vary according to changing trends and circumstances; current policy groups include economic policy; investment and responsible business conduct; taxation; trade; employment and social affairs; corporate governance; biotechnology; and development. Views are exchanged with the OECD Secretariat at all levels, both on policy matters and technical questions. Apart from the annual consultative meeting in the Liaison Committee, BIAC's policy groups meet OECD committees and working parties throughout the year; at staff level, there is almost daily contact.

30. Inasmuch as BIAC brings together the industrial and employers' organizations of OECD member and observer countries, it is thus representative of private enterprise in the most advanced industrialized countries. Thus, BIAC does not necessarily represent all enterprises to which the Guidelines apply, as Guidelines Chapter I on Concepts and Principles, when defining target enterprises, refers to 'ownership [which] may be private, State or mixed'. Following the adoption of the Guidelines in 1976, BIAC has indicated on several occasions that this may constitute a problem since, when considering compliance with the Guidelines, a number of enterprise activities escape BIAC's jurisdiction and involve rather more the responsibility of governments, especially when state-owned enterprises are concerned. While a precise definition of MNEs was never attempted by the OECD Guidelines, this particular issue has been less prominent in recent years.

II. TUAC

31. The Trade Union Advisory Committee to the OECD (TUAC) coordinates and represents the views of the trade union movement in advanced economies, mainly through regular consultations with various OECD committees, the OECD secretariat, and member governments. TUAC sees its role as helping to ensure that global markets are balanced by an effective social dimension. For example, it strongly advocates that support for 'core labour standards' is part of the package in negotiations for expansion of OECD membership. It is also responsible for coordinating the trade union input to the annual G7/G8 economic summits. One of the oldest international trade union groupings enjoying consultative status with an intergovernmental organization, TUAC was founded in 1948 to allow European unions to play a role in the administration of the Marshall Plan by the then OEEC (Organization for European Economic Co-operation) and *vis-à-vis* the European Recovery Programme.[6]

32. With the creation in 1961 of the OEEC's successor, the OECD, TUAC was officially accredited with consultative status by the OECD, representing most of organized labour in OECD member countries. TUAC's affiliates currently consist of about 60 national trade union centres in the 34 OECD member countries which together represent around 70 million workers. Four national organizations from four

6. See TUAC website www.tuac.org; and *Labour and the OECD: the Role of TUAC*, OECD Policy Brief, December 2008, http://www.tuac.org/en/public/tuac/0812_TuacRole.pdf.

non-member countries (Brazil, Indonesia, Russia, South Africa) participate in TUAC work as associates.

33. The large majority of TUAC affiliates are also affiliated to the International Trade Union Confederation (ITUC). Most European affiliates also belong to the European Trade Union Confederation (ETUC). Global union federations (such as the International Metalworkers Federation or Education International) also participate in TUAC work, contributing to it their particular experience of various industrial sectors.

34. TUAC's day-to-day work involves meeting with the OECD Secretariat, committees and member governments to present the views of the trade union movement on the issues on the OECD's agenda. At the same time, TUAC briefs affiliates on a regular basis on the work under way in the OECD, coordinates policy statements on major areas of interest and evaluates the outcome of OECD meetings and publications. The TUAC secretariat, which consists of a General Secretary and several policy advisers, is frequently asked to give presentations to meetings of affiliates and other international trade union organizations.

35. The formal decision-making body within TUAC is the Plenary Session, which meets twice a year. All TUAC affiliates, associate members and global union federation representatives are invited to attend, and usually a large number of trade union Presidents or General Secretaries participate in the meeting. The Plenary Session discusses and approves major policy statements and TUAC's work programme and budget. It also elects an Administrative Committee, which is in charge of overseeing the administration of TUAC and prepares decisions for the Plenary Session on such matters as the budget, membership fees, personnel questions and requests for affiliation.

36. The current (in 2016) President of TUAC is Richard Trumka, President of the AFL-CIO (USA). TUAC has three permanent working groups: on economic policy, on global trade and investment, and on education, training and labour market policy. The working groups prepare TUAC positions for both the Plenary Session and for consultations with the OECD. They are open to all national and international affiliates. Working groups also report on their activities to the Plenary Session. Decisions in all these bodies are, as a rule, made on the basis of consensus, the same principle that applies to decision-making within the OECD as well.

37. TUAC consults regularly with OECD committees and with the bureaux of OECD ministerial meetings where it tends to submit policy statements. As for BIAC, there is also an annual meeting with the OECD Liaison Committee with Non-Governmental Organizations. TUAC as well as BIAC representatives now also participate in some OECD committees or working groups as active observers.

Chapter 2. The OECD Guidelines for Multinational Enterprises: Origins and Main Features

§1. The 1976 Declaration and the Comprehensive 2000 and 2011 Reviews

38. The original Guidelines text of 1976 was annexed to the OECD Ministerial Council Declaration on International Investment and Multinational Enterprises which also contained:

- a commitment by member countries to accord *national treatment* to foreign controlled enterprises operating in their territories. These enterprises should, in exchange for respecting the laws, regulations and administrative practices of their host countries, receive treatment consistent with international law and no less favourable than that accorded in like situations to domestic enterprises;
- a statement on *international investment incentives and disincentives*, whereby member governments recognize the need to strengthen their co-operation in the field of international direct investment and commit themselves to make their official investment incentives and disincentives as transparent as possible;
- a commitment by countries to avoid or minimize *conflicting requirements* imposed on MNEs.

39. The OECD Guidelines were thus conceived as an instrument of international cooperation which was part of a wider framework covering the whole area of international investment and corporate behaviour. They reflected, to an important extent, the concern that the organization of business interests beyond national boundaries can lead to abusive concentrations of power, non-transparent decision-making and conflicts with national policy objectives. Particularly strong concerns still arise in OECD and, even more so, in developing economies, when it is felt that key decisions affecting a local subsidiary are taken elsewhere. The main goal of the Guidelines, therefore, was to encourage MNEs to make positive contribution to economic and social progress, observe advanced standards of responsible business conduct and to minimize and resolve the difficulties and conflicts to which their operations can give rise. Observance of the Guidelines has always been voluntary and is not legally enforceable. This has permitted broad acceptance and contributed to their endorsement by business, although trade unions and NGOs have tended to push for more 'binding' elements and vigorous implementation procedures, thus giving them the 'teeth' they were often seen to lack.

40. The Guidelines have tried to cover the full range of MNE activities, in contrast, for example, to the ILO Tripartite Declaration which refers mainly to labour relations, employment and social policy issues. Thus, the original 1976 text, in addition to an introduction, contained seven chapters on:

- general policies;
- disclosure of information;
- competition;

– financing;
– taxation;
– employment and industrial relations;
– science and technology;

as well as a Council Decision on implementation mechanisms.

41. In the first 25 years, the Guidelines evolved under the impact of periodic reviews by the Investment Committee (then CIME – the Committee for International Investment and Multinational Enterprises), the addition of a new chapter on the Environment (in 1991) and a series of clarifications issued by the committee relating to particular provisions on business conduct. However, by the end of the 1990s, spurred by reports relating to serious violations by some MNEs of core labour rights – such as child labour and freedom of association – public concerns about the impact of increasing flows of foreign investment on the environment, labour standards and human rights were on the increase. There was a widespread view that the OECD Guidelines no longer represented the state of the art for codes of corporate conduct, Further, many critics at the time did not see the implementation mechanisms of the Guidelines as sufficient to counter violations of Guidelines provisions by individual enterprises. TUAC, for example, thought that the lack of effective implementation mechanisms led to cynicism among many concerned parties, that the Guidelines' voluntary character had come to mean 'optional' for many businesses, and that the Committee's clarifications, often 'Kafkaesque', did not help to any measurable degree.[7]

42. Consequently, the June 2000 OECD Ministerial Council adopted an overhauled Guidelines text and a revised Decision on implementation procedures. While the principal features of the Guidelines were maintained – they remained an integral part of the OECD Declaration on International Investment and Multinational Enterprises; and observance by firms remained voluntary – the following decade saw a substantially increased activity by National Contact Points (NCPs). In addition, in comparison with earlier reviews, the changes to the text were far-reaching. With the addition of recommendations relating to the elimination of child and forced labour, all internationally recognized core labour standards were covered by the Guidelines. The environment section encouraged enterprises to raise their environmental performance, through such measures as improved internal environmental management and better contingency planning for environmental impacts. The chapter on disclosure was updated to reflect the OECD Principles on Corporate Governance and enhance firms' social and environmental accountability. In addition, two new chapters – on combating corruption and consumer interests – were added to the text. Further, a recommendation on human rights was introduced in the General Policies section.

7. Statement by John Evans, TUAC General Secretary, to OECD Ministerial Council, 27 June 2000.

43. A decade later, another overhaul was started in May 2010, when the terms of reference for a new update were agreed to by the adhering countries.[8] The update process was concluded in May 2011 with the official adoption of the amendments by the OECD Council. Work on the update included more stakeholders than previously; it was carried out mainly by the Working Party of the Investment Committee, closely assisted by an advisory group of selected government delegates and by representatives from BIAC, TUAC and NGOs (OECD Watch). For work on the update of the Employment and Industrial Relations chapter, the advisory group also relied on representatives from the ILO. Delegates from major non-adhering countries – such as China, India, Indonesia, the Russian Federation and South Africa – were invited to participate in the update process.

44. There were several rationales for starting an update only a decade after the 2000 review. First, countries wanted to ensure the OECD Guidelines' 'continued role as leading international instrument for the promotion of responsible business conduct'. Also, during the previous decade international investment had continued to grow across the globe, but in addition, some of its main features had changed substantially. For example, more complex patterns of production and sourcing had developed and investment from industrialized countries in emerging economies was growing rapidly, at the same time as MNEs from these economies themselves grew in importance. The financial crisis of 2008 and the accompanying loss of confidence in financial policies and fair markets also played a role.

45. The 2011 update resulted in a number of major changes. These included (i) the general principle that firms must address current and potential adverse impacts of their operations, applying 'due diligence'– notably with respect to the management of supply chains and other business relationships – and (ii) the incorporation into the Guidelines of a new full chapter on Human Rights, drawing from the Guiding Principles on Business and Human Rights as developed by the UN Human Rights Council (UNGP). The update also expanded the scope of the Chapter on Employment and Industrial Relations, including its far-reaching alignment with the ILO Tripartite Declaration of Principles on Multinational Enterprises and Social Policy, and renewed and strengthened commitments for environmental standards. Further, implementation procedures were reinforced, *inter alia* by stronger rules governing the handling of complaints through NCPs and by a new focus on peer reviews and peer learning.

46. With the inclusion of the Human Rights chapter in 2011, and after previous reviews had added chapters on the Environment (in 1991) and on combating corruption and consumer interests (in 2000), the Guidelines now contain a preface and 11 individual chapters as summarized below:

---

8. See the terms of reference at http://www.oecd.org/corporate/guidelinesformultinationalenterprises/45124171.pdf.

- The Preface notes the Guidelines' character as laying down principles for responsible business conduct. The common aim of the governments adhering to the Guidelines is to encourage the positive contributions that MNEs can make to economic, environmental and social progress by following appropriate principles and standards of conduct. Adhering governments make a binding commitment to implement these standards.
- Concepts and Principles: sets out the principles which underlie the Guidelines, such as their voluntary character, their application worldwide and the fact that they reflect good practice for all enterprises, multinational or domestic; also specifies the requirement for governments to set up NCPs.
- General Policies: contains the first specific recommendations, including respect for human rights, addressing 'adverse impacts', the need for 'due diligence' in risk management, and provisions on supply chain responsibility, local capacity building, employment creation and training.
- Disclosure: recommends disclosure on all material matters regarding the enterprise such as its performance, governance structure, financial results and ownership, and encourages communication in areas such as compliance with codes of conduct, risk management and social audits.
- Human Rights: requires enterprises to avoid causing or contributing to human rights violations arising from their own activities; to prevent or mitigate adverse human rights impacts linked to products or services by their business relationships; and to carry out 'human rights due diligence', including (i) assessing actual and potential human rights impacts and (ii) taking remedial action.
- Employment and Industrial Relations: addresses major aspects of corporate behaviour in this area, including freedom of association and collective bargaining, child and forced labour, non-discrimination, consultation and cooperation between employers and workers; the need for enterprises to provide adequate wages and working conditions as well as give reasonable notice in cases of plant closure and collective dismissals.
- Environment: encourages enterprises to raise their performance in protecting the environment, and in contributing to the wider goal of sustainable development. An important feature of this chapter concerns the 'precautionary principle' to be followed in combating threats of serious damage to the environment.
- Combating bribery, bribe solicitation and extortion: covers both public and private bribery and addresses passive and active corruption; requests regular monitoring of bribery risks and development of adequate internal controls and compliance programmes.
- Consumer Interests: recommends that enterprises, when dealing with consumers, act in accordance with fair business, marketing and advertising practices, respect consumer privacy, take all reasonable steps to ensure the quality and reliability of goods or services provided, and cooperate with the authorities to combat deceptive marketing practices and prevent threats to public health and safety.
- Science and Technology: aims to promote the rapid diffusion by MNEs of the fruits of research and development activities among the countries where they operate, thereby contributing to sustainable development and the innovative capacities of host countries.

- Competition: emphasizes the importance of an open and competitive business climate; and urges enterprises to refrain from entering into anti-competitive agreements with the aim of, *inter alia*, fixing prices or dividing up market shares.
- Taxation: calls on enterprises to respect both the letter and spirit of tax laws, contribute adequately to the public finances of host countries, avoid inappropriate shifting of profits or losses and to co-operate with tax authorities and provide all information they require.

47. Importantly, starting with the 2000 review, the Investment Committee has supplemented the main text with an extensive commentary to give further explanations to individual provisions. This commentary includes text from previous clarifications provided by the Committee (see §3 below). The main text and commentary, negotiated in the official OECD languages, English and French, have been translated into many other languages. At the beginning of 2016, 46 countries formally adhered to the Guidelines text and implementation provisions, including emerging economies such as Egypt and Peru.[9] Several more non-member countries have applied for adherence, including the Ukraine, Croatia and Serbia.

§2. Main Labour Relations Content: A Brief Overview

48. From the labour and industrial relations point of view, Chapter II on general policies, Chapter III on disclosure of information, Chapter IV on human rights and, evidently, Chapter V on employment and industrial relations are of particular importance within the OECD Guidelines.

49. The general policies chapter makes several recommendations relating to the treatment of workers by a multinational enterprise. First, in contrast with the original 1976 Guidelines, the current version explicitly mentions the respect for internationally recognized human rights.

50. Next, a reference to human capital formation implies that MNEs are encouraged to create employment opportunities and provide adequate training for their existing workforce. The commentary adds that the term also incorporates the notion of non-discrimination in hiring and promotion practices, life-long learning and on-the-job training. If employees engage in *bona fide* 'whistle-blowing' activities, i.e. report practices that they see as contravening national law or standards laid down in the OECD Guidelines to management or public authorities, enterprises are expected to refrain from disciplinary or otherwise discriminatory action.

51. Furthermore, the chapter also includes a 'not lowering standards' provision, which is not only relevant for employment, but also for environmental and other issues. This implies that enterprises should not seek or accept waivers or exemptions from a country's regulatory framework, for example in relation to health,

9. See the list of non-OECD member countries signatory to the Guidelines in paragraph 12 of this monograph.

safety, tax or environmental regulations. For the purpose of the present analysis, this provision is particularly (but not only) relevant for multinationals operating, or envisaging to operate, in lesser developed countries where governments might be inclined to lower certain labour standards when attracting foreign direct investment.[10]

52. Chapter III on disclosure aims to encourage improved information on the operation of MNEs, and their responsiveness to the public's (including employees') increasing demands for transparency. A first set of disclosure recommendations is identical to the disclosure items listed in the OECD Principles of Corporate Governance. Thus, enterprises are recommended to disclose information on all relevant material matters, including the financial situation, company objectives, ownership and foreseeable risk factors. Disclosure of information is also expected on the remuneration of board members and key executives and on 'issues regarding workers and other stakeholders'.

53. A second set of disclosure or communication practices refers to areas where reporting standards are still evolving, such as social, environmental or risk reporting. The commentary to the disclosure chapter notes that many enterprises provide information on topics beyond their financial performance and consider disclosure of such information as a way to show a commitment to socially acceptable practices. Accordingly, the text of the chapter encourages enterprises to draw up codes of conduct or other value statements that would express their commitments in areas such as environmental policies, human rights or labour standards.

54. Chapter IV on human rights elaborates on the more general human rights recommendation in the General Policies chapter, applying this principle not only to an MNE's dealings with its own employees, but also with respect to others affected by its activities. The chapter introduces the concept of 'human rights due diligence', urging enterprises to identify, prevent and/or mitigate actual and potential adverse impacts of their policies, including practices of their suppliers and subcontractors. The commentary refers to the UN Universal Declaration of Human Rights, the UN Framework for Business and Human Rights and its Guiding Principles, and the fundamental labour rights set out in the 1998 ILO Declaration on Fundamental Principles and Rights at Work as being of particular relevance in this regard.[11]

55. The Guidelines Chapter V on employment and industrial relations (more fully discussed in Chapter 4 below) covers the following items:

---

10. The wording 'seek or accept' draws attention to the role of the government in offering such exemptions.
11. Apart from the OECD Guidelines, other international instruments, such as the UN Global Compact, the UN Guiding Principles on Business and Human Rights, the SA 8000 Standard and the Global Reporting Initiative, as well as regional instruments such as the Council of Europe's Convention for the Protection of Human Rights and Fundamental Freedoms, also include references to human rights standards.

- freedom of association and collective bargaining (paras. 1a and b);
- child and forced labour (paras. 1c, d);
- discrimination in employment (para. 1e);
- provision of appropriate facilities to workers' representatives (para. 2a);
- provision of information to employees (paras. 2b and c);
- promotion of consultation and co-operation between employers and employees (para. 3);
- standards of employment and industrial relations, including wages, working conditions and occupational health and safety (para. 4);
- training and employment of local personnel (para. 5);
- reasonable notice and consultation in case of major changes in operations (para. 6);
- unfair influence in bona fide negotiations with employees (para. 7);
- access of employee representatives to real decision makers when negotiating or consulting with management (para. 8).

56. The full text of the chapter, as well as the accompanying commentary, is available in the Codex of this *Encyclopaedia*, under Regional Instruments/OECD. The text is organized in eight paragraphs, one less than in the original 1976 version, due to the integration of a paragraph on non-discrimination (previously para. 7) into paragraph 1. Main substantive textual changes over the original 1976 version are (i) the inclusion of references to two additional core labour standards, i.e. the elimination/abolition of child labour and forced or compulsory labour; (ii) references to joint consultative arrangements between employers and employees; (iii) the addition of text on ensuring occupational health and safety, and on the need for MNEs operating in developing countries to provide adequate wages and working conditions; and (iv) a strengthening of language concerning reasonable advance notice in the case of operational changes with major employment effects, in particular plant closures or mass lay-offs.

57. The commentary situates the recommendations within the broader international discussion of labour standards, with particular reference to ILO instruments (such as the 1998 Declaration on Fundamental Principles and Rights at Work), but adds certain particular perspectives coming out of the negotiations among the signatory countries. It also takes up a number of notions and concepts previously developed in clarifications by the CIME (see the more detailed analysis of the Employment and Industrial Relations Guidelines in Chapter 4 of this monograph below).

§3. Clarifications and 'Specific Instances'

58. The Guidelines apply to businesses from all OECD and other adhering countries, with their diversity of legal systems and regulatory traditions. In addition, the text initially did not contain any commentaries, which were only added in 2000. This has caused difficulties in interpretation of some provisions and a need for clarifying their purpose and intent.

59. When questions arise about corporate conduct, in particular about alleged violations of Guidelines provisions by a certain company, complaints or queries should first be brought to the NCP in the country where the violation is supposed to have occurred. The NCP will offer a forum for discussion, work for an agreement between the parties through consultation, conciliation and mediation – assisted if necessary by NCPs from other countries with a direct interest in the specific case[12] – and thus try to resolve the issue at NCP level. However, if these efforts fail, and in particular if the need for a clarification of a particular guideline is felt, the issue can be submitted to the Investment Committee for consideration.

60. This sequence of events was laid down at an early stage by a Decision of the OECD Council. However, the NCPs had trouble getting off the ground, and many remained more or less dormant during the first two decades. Consequently, a number of issues were raised directly with the Investment Committee (CIME at the time) between 1976 and 2000. The committee then first discussed the need for a clarification. In the affirmative, the resulting clarification referred to how the Guidelines would apply as concerns the issue raised, and to what extent certain practices or types of corporate conduct infringe on the standards contained in them. In other words, the committee used a particular case to clarify the meaning of a provision, and how it should be applied in future cases.[13] By contrast, clarifications were not supposed to be a judgement on the behaviour of a particular enterprise, which was therefore never referred to by name in corresponding CIME statements or press releases. Only after 2000 did NCPs develop a status strong enough to make it unnecessary for complainants to immediately turn to the Committee. The 2011 Decision of the Council confirms the Committee's function in clarifying the Guidelines, but only in cases where an adhering country or an advisory body makes a submission to the Committee questioning whether an NCP has correctly handled a complaint case ('specific instance').[14]

I. Clarifications by the Investment Committee, 1976–2000

61. Thirty-five complaint cases (officially called 'requests for clarification') were brought to the attention of CIME between the adoption of the Guidelines in 1976 and the revision in 2000, about half of which resulted in clarifications. Of these 24 were brought by TUAC, while 5 cases in all were introduced by the Belgian government, 2 by the Netherlands, and 1 each by the Danish, French and UK governments. One case (the closure of Renault Vilvoorde in 1997) was introduced jointly by France and Belgium. None was introduced by the Business and Industry Advisory Committee. The vast majority of cases (30) were brought during

12. As an example, the NCP of the country where the alleged violation is supposed to have happened is likely to cooperate with the NCP of the country where the relevant MNE is headquartered.
13. For Salzmann (2000, p. 791), this is as if the US Congress, or another parliamentary body, continued creating legislative history after passage of a statute.
14. The corresponding mechanism at the ILO is the Interpretation procedure at the ILO's Governing Body. However, there is no correspondence at the ILO to the OECD's implementation mechanism via National Contact Points.

the first decade after the adoption of the Guidelines; the last case brought (by TUAC) directly to the Committee in 1999 involved bargaining issues at the Australian multinational Rio Tinto.

62. The individual requests to CIME up to the 2000 review and the issues they involved are listed below.[15] These complaint cases and the clarifications that followed, laid an important basis for interpreting the text and solving complaints, although some clarifications have been overtaken by events, including economic developments and the periodic revisions to the Guidelines text. However, over time complaints became less numerous, first since the Investment Committee indeed successfully clarified provisions that may have been in doubt, but also since, in particular, trade unions grew disenchanted with the sometimes obscure pronouncements of the Committee and with what they interpreted the lack of 'teeth' of the Guidelines implementation process. After the 2000 review, the number of cases raised (about 350 between 2000 and 2015, now designated as 'specific instances') has again considerably increased, but *nota bene*, these have been raised and handled at the level of NCPs, and not the Committee itself.

A. *Issues Raised in the late 1970s*

63. These include:

- the co-responsibility of the parent company and subsidiaries: the Badger case;
- trade union rights: Motor Iberica, Spanish subsidiary of Massey Ferguson;
- trade union recognition by the multinational subsidiary of Black and Decker in the UK;
- Philips, Netherlands: permission for leave of absence for participation at an international trade union seminar on developments within Philips, and meetings with trade unions at world level;
- adequacy of information by the French multinational Poclain in a situation of economic difficulties, mass dismissals and possibility of takeover;
- international structural reorganization, loss of employment and job guarantees based on state subsidies at the Dutch Bendix subsidiary;
- closure of the Siemens plant in Belgium and employment commitments between Siemens and the Belgian government;
- policy of Warner-Lambert to close down its operation in Sweden, against the background of comparable standards of employment;
- production transfer with plant closure in Sweden by Litton Industries;
- Philips, Germany: information of the trade unions and cooperation with them on plant closures;

15. For a discussion of the cases handled by CIME up to 1985, see R. Blanpain, *The OECD Guidelines for Multinational Enterprises and Labour Relations, 1976–1979. Experience and Review*, Kluwer 1979; *1979–1982, Experience and Midterm Report*, 1983; and *1982–1984. Experience and Review Report*, 1985. For detailed language from CIME clarifications based on cases up to 1994, see OECD, *The OECD Guidelines for Multinational Enterprises*, Paris 1994.

- changes in company structure by International Telephone and Telegraph Corporation (ITT) in Germany, and their repercussions on trade union information and participation;
- alleged worldwide anti-union policy by Citibank-Citicorp;
- the transfer of staff across borders during a labour dispute (Hertz);
- status of European airline groupings, such as KSSU or Atlas, as MNEs;
- transfer of a profit-making subsidiary to another country: British American Tobacco Company BATCO;
- closing down of subsidiary by Firestone; access to the real decision-makers.

B. Issues Raised in the 1980s

64. These include:

- airline groupings (continued); status as MNEs, adequacy of consultation;
- access to real decision makers: Viggo-British Oxygen case;
- information and consultation of employees in case of plant closure at Philips-Finland.
- information and consultation of employees in case of plant closure; access to real decision makers: Ford Motor Co. Amsterdam;
- reasonable notice: generic issue raised by Belgian government.
- the right of employees to be represented: Norsk Hydro; Qantas Airlines; National Association of Manufacturers (USA);
- the use of national languages at Citibank (Denmark);
- status as multinational enterprise; information on the group as a whole: C&A Brenninkmayer;
- structural adaptation: the Hyster case.
- reasonable notice in case of redundancy: Bankers Trust;
- disclosure of information (true and fair view): generic case raised by Belgium;
- conflict with national priorities, and reasonable notice in case of plant closure: Michelin (France).
- pay and employment standards inferior to 'comparable employers': Food Lion (USA).

C. Issues Raised in the 1990s

65. These include:

- reasonable notice; complete transfer of production activity: Hoover-Europe;
- reasonable notice in case of plant closure: Belgian metal-working company;
- reasonable notice in case of plant closure; relation between parent company and local entity: Renault Vilvoorde;
- replacement of collective bargaining by individual contracts; compliance with national law: Rio Tinto (Australia).

II. Complaints with National Contact Points after 2000

66. As indicated, since the 2000 review complaint cases are no longer directly submitted to the Committee. Rather, the about 360 'specific instances' raised between 2000 and 2015 and registered in the OECD's official database – the highest number having been raised in the UK and the US (with over 40 cases each), followed by Germany – were handled by the NCPs, whose role in the resolution of grievances was strengthened decisively in the 2000 update. In the OECD count, trade unions and NGOs filed about 300 cases altogether, while the rest were filed by individuals, business (only 4 cases) and other interested parties. A breakdown by host country show that most cases occurred in the US, the Democratic Republic of the Congo, Brazil and India. More detail on current implementation procedures can be found in Chapter 5 of this monograph.

67. Issues raised since 2000 have continued to deal predominantly with the Chapter on Employment and Industrial Relations, although in recent years the General Policies, Human Rights and Environment chapters have gained in importance, accompanied by a rise in the share of complaints submitted by NGOs.[16] By 2016, however, employment and industrial relations issues still constituted almost three out of every five cases ever brought to NCPs. The industrial sectors most involved were, in that order, manufacturing, mining, financial activities and trade, although since the 2011 update, financial and insurance activities have passed manufacturing industry as the sector with the largest number of specific instances. A number of industrial relations cases have related to alleged anti-union campaigns or refusal to bargain by management, and to lack of information and belated notice in case of plant closures or production transfers. The number of cases dealing with company activities in non-adhering countries has increased significantly, representing between 2011 and 2015 about half of the total (more detail can be found in the OECD's Annual Guidelines Reports).

68. TUAC and OECD Watch publish their own accounts of cases brought by trade unions and NGOs, and totals may differ from the OECD Secretariat's own calculations (which tend to be lower since they rely on NCPs' sometimes incomplete reporting, particularly in the early years after 2000, and have tended not to include complaints not accepted for consideration).[17] The TUAC website in early 2016 lists 172 specific instances as originating from trade union complaints. Naturally, there is a correlation between cases raised by unions and alleged violations of the Employment and Industrial Relations chapter. A TUAC analysis notes that union cases originated in 30 OECD and other adhering countries, and in 33 non-adhering countries. In the latter group, Burma, Sri Lanka and India had the highest number of cases while, in the former, it was Brazil and the United States. As to industrial

---

16. Since the 2011 review Human Rights has been the chapter most cited in complaints cases. See OECD, *Annual Report on the OECD Guidelines for Multinational Enterprises 2013*, p. 46; 2014, p. 41; 2016, p. 32.
17. In fact, in late 2015, trade union and NGO websites report altogether over 420 specific instances submitted. This figure may include double counting, as some complaints are brought jointly by trade unions and NGOs.

sectors referred to in these complaints, the three industries with the highest number of union complaints were (a) food, agriculture and tobacco; (b) the automobile industry: and (c) textiles, leather and garments.[18]

69. However, the weight of civil society organizations in the process is increasing, and in recent years the majority of cases was indeed raised by NGOs. OECD Watch notes that, as of June 2015, 250 Guidelines cases had been filed by NGOs, communities and individuals (which includes rejected cases), over a third of which filed since 2012. Classified by issue (not chapter) about 75 per cent of the complaints concerned Human Rights, 50 per cent concerned impacts by business relations (i.e. mainly supply chain issues), followed by the environment and labour rights (multiple listings possible).[19]

70. Many of these Guidelines cases are in areas that go to the heart of the debate on the social impacts of globalization, including trade union recognition, human rights issues, child and forced labour and the social implications of the exploitation of natural resources. A certain number of relevant cases are mentioned below.

71. Freedom-of-association issues have been raised on a large number of occasions. Complaints about anti-union campaigns, lack of trade union recognition for bargaining purposes, etc., are recurrent. For example, in 2008, trade unions complained that at a Unilever factory in Pakistan had terminated the contracts of a large number of temporary workers seeking permanent status, within a context of intimidation and with the direct aim of preventing union membership. The UK NCP was able to find a solution to this conflict through conciliation. In another case in 2008, trade unions submitted a case against Nestle Indonesia (a subsidiary of Nestle Switzerland), claiming that the company did not respect the rights of the local trade union and refused to engage in collective bargaining, in particular on wages. The Swiss NCP undertook mediation meetings with all parties involved and closed the case (considered premature by the trade union since not all issues raised had been addressed) when notified that the company and the union had reached agreement to include wages in the next bargaining round.

72. A major case of reasonable notice in 2001/02 was that of the closing of outlets in several European countries by the Marks & Spencer store chain, which was taken up by the French and Belgian NCPs. In a similar case, the UK NCP found that PSA Peugeot did not fully follow the Guidelines 'reasonable notice' principle when closing down its Ryton manufacturing plant in 2006; in particular, 'the Company should have engaged with the Unions when the decision to make the closure of Ryton was at a formative stage'. The 40 or so trade union cases brought between

18. If all of its subsectors were added together, the manufacturing sector would have the largest share, as in the OECD's count above. As of 1 January, 2016, 92 per cent of all trade union complaints concerned Chapter V, followed by 29 per cent referring to Chapter II (multiple listings possible), see TUAC, *Trade Union Cases, Key Statistics*, www.tuacoecdmneguidelines.org/statistics.asp. According to the OECD count of all cases submitted, 56 per cent concerned Chapter V issues, see OECD Database of specific instances, http://mneguidelines.oecd.org/database/.
19. OECD Watch, *Quarterly Case Update*, Vol 10, No. 1, June 2015.

2010 and 2015 include interference with the right to organize (Starbucks in Chile; Nissan in the US; METRO in Pakistan), alleged abusive use of contract labour and precarious employment relationships (Mondelez in Pakistan; Pepsico in India), dismissal without consultation in a Brazilian bank, and factory closures in Italy (Eaton), France (Molex) and Brazil (Unilever). According to the TUAC case listing, only a minority of these cases were decided to the satisfaction of the complainants. For example, of the aforementioned cases, Nissan refused the mediation offer, and Starbucks withdrew from the process due to a perceived lack of impartiality of the NCP, but later agreed bilaterally to wage increases and recognition of trade union activities.

73. Child labour cases are still recurring and are brought both by trade unions and NGOs. In a case in 2001, the Netherlands NCP looked into allegations by an NGO (India Committee of the Netherlands) of the use of child labour in outsourcing operations in India by the sporting goods company Adidas. In this case, the NCP found that Adidas had encouraged its suppliers to operate in a socially responsible manner. In 2004, NGOs complained that Bayer Crop Science used suppliers that employed children in cotton picking. The NCP closed the instance after Bayer pledged to combat child labour more actively, including liaising with suppliers on the issue. In 2008, the UK NCP issued a very strong condemnation of Afrimex operating in the Democratic Republic of Congo, for failing to respect human rights and to take adequate steps to contribute to the abolition of child and forced labour.

74. Cases involving investment in Myanmar, where forced labour has been found to be widespread, have been raised at several NCPs in the early to mid-2000s. Following enquiries by labour unions on companies' operations there, the French NCP issued recommendations in 2002 of practices that companies can use to contribute to the fight against forced labour. It also noted that such practices cannot be a substitute for the enforcement of government measures necessary to suppress forced labour.[20]

75. Another issue is the adverse impact on populations of the exploitation of natural resources by MNEs. In 2001, the Canadian NCP was asked by NGOs to consider the impending removal of local farmers from a Canadian mining company's lands in Zambia and encouraged the company to cooperate with Canadian and Zambian NGOs in reconsidering the company's resettlement plans. In 2012, the French trade union CGT and four NGOs submitted a specific instance to the French NCP alleging that the Michelin tyre company, by constructing a factory in Tamil Nadu, India, was destroying the livelihood of the local community. The NCP Final Statement described an 'ongoing stalemate between the parties' but noted that the Michelin Group had undertaken work for an environmental, societal and human rights study, and that it had committed to the development of a subsequent action plan to adapt its CSR policy and internal due diligence systems in response to the outcomes of the study.

---

20. See Recommendations by the French National Contact Point to Companies on the Issue of Forced Labour in Burma, 28 March 2002, http://www.tresor.economie.gouv.fr/File/372056.

76. The NCP called on Michelin to take into account the recommendations contained in its Final Statement, which also provided for NCP follow-up on the implementation of its recommendations. Michelin has subsequently sent the NCP regular updates on its implementation of the NCP's recommendations.[21]

77. More information on most of these 'specific instances' can be found in various OECD publications, such as the OECD's annual reports on the Guidelines,[22] the websites of NCPs, as well as continuously updated lists by TUAC, OECD Watch and the OECD itself. The OECD Database of specific instances, referred to above, contains information on specific instances by country, theme, date and other criteria. However, for a well-rounded picture on a specific case, it is useful to consult the trade union and OECD Watch websites as well.

---

21. See OECD, Annual Report on the OECD Guidelines for Multinational Enterprises 2014; the TUAC case register under http://www.tuacoecdmneguidelines.org/; and various statements by the French NCP under http://www.tresor.economie.gouv.fr/5731_Les-communiques-du-PCN.
22. See for example *OECD Guidelines for Multinational Enterprises. Focus on Responsible Supply Chain Management, Annual Report 2002*, Paris 2002; *Annual Report on the OECD Guidelines for Multinational Enterprises 2008, Employment and Industrial Relations,* Paris 2008; or *Annual Report on the OECD Guidelines for Multinational Enterprises 2014, Responsible Business Conduct by Sector,* Paris 2014.

Chapter 3. Some Broader Issues

§1. The Definition of a Multinational Enterprise

78. Chapter I on concepts and principles notes that a precise definition of MNEs is not required for the purposes of the Guidelines. The chapter nevertheless goes on to provide a broad type of definition, i.e. they 'usually comprise companies or other entities established in more than one country and so linked that they may co-ordinate their operations in various ways'. The chapter also acknowledges that the degree of autonomy of the various units constituting an MNE may vary widely from one MNE to another; in addition, ownership may be private, state or mixed. Importantly, 'the Guidelines are addressed to all the entities within the multinational enterprise (parent companies and/or local entities)'.

79. The Guidelines text thus acknowledges that the concept of MNE embraces a diversity of situations found throughout the business world. For example, early clarifications by CIME have confirmed that majority ownership is not the exclusive form of linkage between two companies in different countries which may be considered part of an MNE.

80. Importantly, the original 1976 text which noted as one characteristic of MNEs that one or more of its companies 'may be able to exercise a significant influence over the activities of others' was much softened in later revisions, and the current text refers only to entities 'so linked that they may coordinate their operations in various ways'. This acknowledges that in today's MNEs the element of central control and centralized decision-making is often much less prominent. More generally, with the increased importance of strategic alliances and closer relations with suppliers and contractors, they encompass a broader range of organizational forms than previously.

81. Finally, as noted in paragraph 5 of Chapter I on concepts and principles, the Guidelines are not aimed at introducing differences of treatment between MNEs and domestic enterprises; 'they reflect good practice for all'. Accordingly, multinational and domestic enterprises are subject to the same expectations from adhering governments. This rule of equal treatment is inspired by a strong political will not to discriminate between national and MNEs, which resulted in the inclusion of the 'national treatment' principle in the original 1976 Declaration of the Council, as well as subsequently revised versions.

§2. The Voluntary Character of the Guidelines

82. The Guidelines are recommendations jointly addressed by governments to MNEs operating in their territories. They lay down standards for the activities of MNEs and, where relevant, of national enterprises in the different adhering countries. As noted in the preface to the Guidelines, their observance is voluntary and not legally enforceable. They provide voluntary principles and standards for responsible business conduct, as recommended to enterprises by OECD and other adhering governments. In fact, even among OECD member countries any attempt to establish a binding code of conduct would remain illusory.

83. However, 'voluntary' does not imply that MNEs are completely free to choose whether they accept the Guidelines or not. The Guidelines constitute recommended behaviour, addressed by adhering countries to the MNEs; thus, they carry the weight of a firm expectation of governments for MNE behaviour. In addition, adhering countries make a binding commitment to implement the principles laid down in the instrument through the set-up of appropriate machinery. Further, both BIAC and TUAC, representing dozens of industry and trade union associations, have accepted the Guidelines as the appropriate behaviour to expect from enterprises. This strongly suggests that the Guidelines constitute important rules of conduct which society as a whole expects MNEs to live up to – even though it remains true that no legal proceedings can be initiated on their basis in either national or international courts.

84. Difficult questions arise concerning the relationship between the obligations and standards of behaviour that the Guidelines impose, and the legal obligations under the law of the land. Every state has the right to prescribe the conditions under which MNEs operate within its national jurisdiction, subject to international law and the international agreements to which it subscribes. The current Guidelines text notes – which is indeed self-evident – that 'Obeying domestic laws is the first obligation of enterprises. The Guidelines are not a substitute for nor should they be considered to override domestic law and regulation' (Chapter I).

85. Situations may sometimes arise where enterprises face conflicting requirements between domestic law and Guidelines standards. In this case, 'enterprises should seek ways to honor such principles and standards to the fullest extent which does not place them in violation of domestic law' (Chapter I). In sum, national law comes first, confirming the sovereignty of the state; and consequently, the Guidelines cannot induce enterprises to do anything which would be in conflict with national law.

86. However, the Guidelines do place obligations on multinationals which go beyond what is strictly required by national law. If they demanded merely that multinationals must respect national law, they would be superfluous. In fact, they were developed against the background that national law does not suffice to regulate the 'transnational' character of the multinational phenomenon. Consequently the Guidelines may add obligations and are thus supplementary to national law. For example, the so-called 'chapeau' clause of the Chapter on Employment and Industrial Relations reads 'Enterprises should, within the framework of applicable law, regulations and prevailing labour relations and employment practices and applicable international labour standards ...', which implies, first, that national legal systems need to be taken into account and, second, that the application of national law is not in itself sufficient. The text can indeed go further than national legislation, for example when stating (in paragraph 6 of the Employment and Industrial Relations chapter) that a reasonable term of notice, 'prior to the final decision being taken', of important business changes must be given to employees – even if no such notice was obligatory under national law.

87. At this point, it should be noted that a complaining party that has requested NCP mediation, may also have brought its case before the national legal system. Up to the 2011 update, many NCPs rejected such 'parallel proceedings' and refused to consider cases ('specific instances') that were already handled in the courts. Only in the 2011 update did the Investment Committee introduce a clause to the effect that the existence or preparation of such parallel proceedings should not prevent NCPs from taking on a specific instance. Nevertheless, some NCPs have continued to automatically reject cases submitted to ordinary courts.

88. Finally, the Guidelines also recommend the use of appropriate international dispute settlement mechanisms, including arbitration, as a means of facilitating the resolution of legal problems arising between enterprises and member countries (Guidelines, Chapter I, para. 10).

§3. Responsibilities of the Various Entities of a Multinational Enterprise

89. Of course, parent–subsidiary relationships with strong control of the parent company continue to exist, and CIME clarifications on the responsibilities of the various entities of a multinational enterprise have acknowledged this situation:

> All entities, including parent companies, local subsidiaries, as well as intermediary levels of the organization, are expected to co-operate and assist, as necessary, in observing the Guidelines. To the extent that parent companies actually exercise control over the activities of their subsidiaries, they have a responsibility for observance of the Guidelines by those subsidiaries. Consultation between the parent and its local entities would undoubtedly assist in achieving the purposes of the Guidelines. As long as enterprises can ensure this co-operation and assistance, it would be up to the various entities to decide the division of responsibilities between parent companies and local entities ...

90. The Guidelines obviously expect that all entities will cooperate to ensure their observance. The Committee, therefore, has suggested that 'a "prudent enterprise" would set up whatever internal procedures would be necessary to ensure that the Guidelines are known and applied by its various entities'.

91. The concept of responsibilities of the various entities of a multinational enterprise – including the problem of the co-responsibility of the parent company for the obligations of its subsidiaries – is important for several of the Guidelines chapters. For example, Chapter III on disclosure addresses the parent company directly when referring to the fact that 'information should be disclosed for the enterprise as a whole and, where appropriate, along business lines or geographic areas' (paragraph 1).

92. In the Employment and Industrial Relations chapter, paragraphs 2, 6 and 8 are of particular importance in this regard. Following paragraph 2c, workers and their representatives should receive all necessary information to enable them to obtain a 'true and fair view of the performance of the entity or, where appropriate, the enterprise as a whole'. This implies that, where employee representatives experience difficulties in obtaining such information at national level, other entities of the enterprise (in particular the parent company or headquarters) are called for to provide local management with the necessary information so as to enable local managers to comply with this particular paragraph.

93. Paragraph 6 recommends that MNEs, when considering operational changes with major employment effects, such as company or establishment closures, provide reasonable notice of such changes to workers and their representatives, as well as to relevant governmental authorities. It is self-evident that here also the parent company or MNE-headquarters must inform local management in due time so that they can provide the 'reasonable notice of such changes' as required by this Guideline.

94. Finally, paragraph 8, which sets the principle of access to the real decision makers, provides that MNEs should enable worker representatives to conduct negotiations or consultations with representatives of management, who are authorized to take decisions on the matters under negotiation. Clearly, therefore, the MNE must delegate sufficient authority to the local level or else involve negotiators from the parent company provided with decision-making authority.

95. Equally important is the problem of the financial responsibility of the parent company for certain financial obligations of its subsidiaries. Following the Badger case in the late 1970s[23] – where Badger Belgium, a subsidiary of the US based company of the same name, went out of business without offering sufficient compensation to its dismissed workers – the CIME has stated that the Guidelines:

> do not imply an unqualified principle of parent company responsibility. Nonetheless, in certain cases, parent companies have assumed on a voluntary basis financial responsibility for a subsidiary, and such behaviour may actually be considered good management practice under the Guidelines. This question is especially relevant when discussing changes in the operations of a firm and co-operation between the entities to mitigate resulting adverse effects.

96. In sum, the various items of Guidelines text cited above on the co-responsibility of the parent for the affiliate, as well as the Committee's conclusions on the subject, are again suggestive of the fact that the OECD Guidelines have

23. See R. Blanpain, *The Badger Case and the OECD Guidelines for Multinational Enterprises*, Deventer, Kluwer, 1977.

established standards of behaviour and responsibilities for MNEs that can go beyond national law.

§4. MNEs' Consistency with National Policies

97. The general policies chapter provides that enterprises should 'take fully into account established policies in the countries in which they operate'. In its 1979 review report of the first three years of experience with the Guidelines, the OECD pointed out the relevance of this proviso in cases of closure of a local subsidiary of a multinational enterprise, noting that, while enterprises retain the right of cutting back on their workforce or closing down a business, a prudent company should seek clarification of government policies through advance consultations with the government concerned. This concrete recommendation has not been retained in the current commentary to the chapter; instead, the text encourages companies to 'co-operate with governments in the development and implementation of policies and laws'.

§5. Geographical Scope

98. The Guidelines are addressed to the MNEs operating on the territories of adhering governments, but Chapter I makes clear that they apply to MNE activities 'wherever they operate' (paragraph 3). There is thus the firm expectation by adhering governments that MNEs apply the Guidelines standards worldwide. In other words, the Guidelines fully apply to MNEs operating in non-adhering countries, and in fact it is here where their global effectiveness is particularly at stake.

99. It can be argued that in developing countries the Guidelines' worldwide applicability can help supplement gaps which may exist in local legislation or serve as a model for new laws and regulations. From the point of view of non-OECD economies, the application of worldwide standards by MNEs may provide direct benefits in terms of improved working conditions or environmental protection, and not the least through their demonstration effects for local companies. Suitable arrangements for cooperation with non-members who do not adhere to the Guidelines are important in this context: first, to make it impossible for companies to avoid the Guidelines' recommendations simply by outsourcing to those countries; and second, to counter claims of discrimination or distortion of competition since OECD-based MNEs are expected to follow the Guidelines recommendations in countries whose enterprises might be subject to less demanding laws and expectations. In this context, it should be noted that complaints can be submitted also from non-adhering countries, and trade unions and NGOs operating in such countries have done so in increasing numbers.

§6. Business Partners and Supply-chain Management

100. Do the OECD Guidelines refer only to *investment* or also to other activities, such as *trade*? In particular, the question arises as to whether the text applies also to subcontractors and outsourcing practices. Should an MNE assume responsibility for the observance of standards by its subcontractors? While already in the 1990s certain voluntary company codes started to entail some form of obligation for contractors and subcontractors to live up to the employment standards set out by them, BIAC and other business associations, but also many government representatives in the Investment Committee, tended to maintain for a long time that the Guidelines refer exclusively to investment activities – considering that they are part of the OECD Declaration on International Investment and Multinational Enterprises. By contrast, the trade unions and NGOs have long favoured a broader view of their relevance, and started in the early 2000s to bring cases before NCPs that involve trade relationships with suppliers.[24]

101. A perspective involving broader business relationships was introduced into the Guidelines text in 2000, by asking enterprises to 'encourage, where practicable, business partners, including suppliers and subcontractors, to apply principles of corporate conduct compatible with the Guidelines' (Chapter II). This clause was included against the background that MNEs had evolved to encompass a broad range of business arrangements, with new sourcing strategies and many different forms of influence or control over subsidiaries, suppliers and contractors.

102. The Investment Committee pointed out at the time that there was room for flexibility in assessing the presence or not of an investment relationship in the supply chain. In this context, it argued that the number of suppliers or other business partners, the 'market power' of the enterprise *vis-à-vis* its business partners, and the existence of market arrangements designed to ensure supplier accountability for particular aspects of performance (such as product quality) played an important role.

103. Further, in June 2003 the Committee issued a policy statement on the Guidelines' scope, a kind of clarification without carrying that precise designation, noting first the foundation of the instrument in an 'investment nexus'. However, it went on by pointing out the crucial issue of 'the practical ability of enterprises to influence the conduct of their business partners with whom they have an investment-like relationship. In considering Recommendation 2.10 [of the 2000 Guidelines version], a case-by-case approach is warranted that takes account of all factors relevant to the nature of the relationship and the degree of influence.'

24. For example, NGOs noted their position at an OECD Conference that 'when companies contract directly with suppliers, but fail to use their influence on those suppliers' respect of labour rights, these companies are complicit in the human rights violations suffered by workers' (*OECD Guidelines for Multinational Enterprises: Focus on Responsible Supply Chain Management*, Annual Report 2002, Paris 2002, p. 68). In the 2011 update, this position found widespread support.

104. The 2011 update retains the recommendation that MNEs encourage their business partners to apply Guidelines principles, but goes much further and clearly requests MNEs to assume more responsibility concerning the observance of standards by their business partners. The Guidelines now ask MNEs to 'seek to prevent or mitigate an adverse impact', even if they have not themselves contributed to that impact, but when it is nevertheless 'directly linked to their operations, products or services by a business relationship'. MNEs are asked to carry out 'risk-based due diligence', as part of their enterprise risk management system, to prevent and mitigate such adverse impacts (Chapter II).

105. The commentary provides further guidance on this point by pointing out that:

> To avoid causing or contributing to adverse impacts ... includes their activities in the supply chain. Relationships in the supply chain take a variety of forms including, for example, franchising, licensing or subcontracting... In the context of its supply chain, if the enterprise identifies a risk of causing an adverse impact, then it should take the necessary steps to cease or prevent that impact ... if the enterprise identifies a risk of contributing to an adverse impact, then it should take the necessary steps to cease or prevent its contribution and use its leverage to mitigate any remaining impacts ...

106. Leverage is defined as an enterprise's 'ability to effect change in the wrongful practices of the entity that causes the harm'. Obviously, the extent of leverage varies with a number of factors, such as product characteristics, the number of suppliers, structural characteristics of the supply chain, and how crucial the business partner is to the multinational enterprise. Depending on the extent of leverage and the crucial or otherwise relationship between the entities, the Guidelines commentary offers as potential response to adverse impact (i) the continuation of the relationship with the partner while undertaking efforts at risk mitigation; (ii) temporary suspension of the relationship during efforts at risk mitigation; or (iii) disengagement with the supplier where mitigation fails or where the adverse impact is considered too severe.

107. The 2011 OECD Roundtable of NCPs summarized the long trajectory from 'investment only' to 'multiple business relationships' by confirming that the 'due diligence/supply chain approach ... extends the scope of the application of the Guidelines from investment to business relationships, including suppliers, agents and franchises and makes due diligence a part of the overall business risk-management tools'.[25]

---

25. *Annual Report on the OECD Guidelines for Multinational Enterprises 2011: A New Agenda for the Future*, Paris 2011, p. 198.

§7. Human Rights and Due Diligence

108. The issue of business and human rights was long hidden behind the responsibility of governments/states for human rights. Efforts at the United Nations to create standards for enterprises' human rights obligations were crowned with success only in June 2011, when the UN Human Rights Council endorsed the Guiding Principles on Business and Human Rights (UNGP).[26]

109. The OECD Guidelines have incorporated a reference to corporate responsibility for Human Rights since the 2000 update. The new full Human Rights Chapter adopted in 2011 draws upon the UN 'Protect, Respect and Remedy' framework and urges enterprises to respect the Human Rights as set out in (a) the Universal Declaration of Human Rights; (b) the International Covenant on Civil and Political Rights; (c) the International Covenant on Economic, Social and Cultural Rights; and (d) the ILO Declaration on Fundamental Principles and Rights at Work. It requires enterprises to avoid causing or contributing to human rights violations arising from their own activities (which can include both actions and omissions) and address such violations when they occur. In addition, enterprises should prevent or mitigate adverse human rights impacts linked to products or services by their business relationships, even if they do not themselves contribute to those impacts.

110. Further, in paragraph 5 of the chapter MNEs are held to carry out 'human rights due diligence', defined as a process that 'entails assessing actual and potential human rights impacts, integrating and acting upon the findings, tracking responses as well as communicating how impacts are addressed'. The level of due diligence should be driven, *inter alia*, by the size of the enterprise and the severity of actual and potential adverse impacts.[27]

111. The Guidelines also stipulate that enterprises clearly profess a public policy commitment to respect human rights and have processes in place to enable remediation when having caused or contributed to an adverse impact. However, they refrain from defining the exact nature of such remedies. By contrast, they point out in some detail that MNEs need to consider additional Human Rights standards in cases where adverse impacts concern individuals belonging to specific groups or populations, such as indigenous peoples, ethnic or religious minorities, women, children, persons with disabilities or migrants.

112. Just like the UN Guiding Principles, the Guidelines recognize the primary obligation of states to respect and protect Human Rights and fundamental freedoms. But what happens when a state either fails to enforce relevant laws and standards or

---

26. See Human Rights Council, Report of the Special Representative of the Secretary-General on the issue of human rights and transnational corporations and other business enterprises, John Ruggie, 21 March 2011; and http://www.business-humanrights.org/Documents/UNGuidingPrinciples.

27. See TUAC, *The OECD Guidelines for Multinational Enterprises*, 2012, Figure 2.5, for an attempt to operationalize the concept of human rights due diligence in terms of actions expected from enterprises.

even acts contrary to them? The commentary to the human rights chapter makes it very clear that this:

> does not diminish the expectation that enterprises respect human rights. In countries where domestic laws and regulations conflict with internationally recognized human rights, enterprises should seek to honor them to the fullest extent which does not place them in violation of domestic law ...

§8. Weak Governance Zones and High-risk Areas

113. Based on its work on the Guidelines, the INV Committee has developed several instruments to tackle the issue of enterprise behaviour in weak governance zones and areas affected by armed conflict. These are environments where governments are unable or unwilling to assume their roles in protecting basic rights. The OECD Risk Awareness Tool for Multinational Enterprises in Weak Governance Zones, adopted by the OECD Council in June 2006, attempts to promote responsible business conduct when investing in such areas and, in particular, help avoid the illegal exploitation of natural resources in areas of armed conflict.

114. Further, in 2011 the OECD Council issued a Recommendation on Due Diligence Guidance for Responsible Supply Chains of Minerals from Conflict-affected and High-risk Areas. This Guidance was developed, in particular, on the basis of the experience of the Great Lakes Region in Africa, in cooperation with 11 countries of the region and the United Nations. Recognizing the serious abuses associated with the extraction, transport and trade in 'conflict minerals' (tin, tantulum, tungsten and gold), it aims to guide companies in respecting human rights and recommends that they follow a five-step framework for risk-based due diligence in the mineral supply chain.[28]

§9. Garment and Footwear Supply Chains

115. Following on from the instruments noted above on due diligence in high risk areas, and in particular after the collapse of the Rana Plaza building in Dhaka, Bangladesh in 2013, NCPs and the OECD Secretariat have also been active in strengthening the Guidelines in garment and footwear supply chains and develop due diligence guidance to enterprises active in the sector.

---

28. *OECD Risk Awareness Tool for Multinational Enterprises in Weak Governance Zones*, Paris 2006; *OECD Due Diligence Guidance for Responsible Supply Chains of Minerals from Conflict-affected and High-risk Areas*, 2nd edn, Paris 2013, and 3rd edn, Paris 2016. 'Weak Governance Zones and Conflict-Affected and High-Risk Areas', Ch. 5 in *Annual Report on the OECD Guidelines for Multinational Enterprises 2011*. With reference to the Due Diligence Guidance, the US Securities and Exchange Commission is requesting of companies investing in the area an annual listing of measures taken to undertake due diligence on the source and chain of custody of 'conflict minerals'.

116. The garment and footwear sector is characterized by high labour intensity, low added value and strong price competition. Social and environmental risk factors may therefore arise at all subcontracting levels, such as child labour, forced labour, cascade contracting, excessive overtime and lack of payment for it, restrictions to union formation, etc. In response to these risk factors, and the multiple accidents that have occurred, numerous initiatives have been developed on the national and multilateral level to combat dangerous working conditions in textile supply chains. Many buyers, too, have developed more careful and comprehensive diligence management systems on their own.

117. NCP meetings confirmed that the Guidelines recommendation in Chapter II to carry out 'risk-based due diligence' and identify potential or real 'adverse impact' fully applies to the sector, and in particular two reports on the subject were issued by the French and Italian NCPs, which outlined concrete measures expected from enterprises.[29] Subsequently, the Secretariat and the INV Committee jointly developed a Due Diligence Guidance for Responsible Supply Chains in the Garment and Footwear Sector, to be published in the course of 2016. Among other things, the publication lists the due diligence expected from enterprises in the area of labour and industrial relations, such as to:

- identify and prevent anti-trade union policies and acivities within their supply chain;
- use their leverage with suppliers to prevent such policies and, if necessary, suspend orders or discontinue their engagement;
- assess all suppliers operating at stage 1 and possibly beyond in high-risk countries as to whether their wage payment complies with national law and satisfies the basic need of workers and their families.

In addition, the Secretariat and the INV Committee are currently (2016) finalizing similar guidance for extractive industries and for the financial sector. Furthermore, the OECD and the Food and Agriculture Organisation of the United Nations have published jointly a guide for responsible supply chains in agriculture.

29. See Statement by the National Contact Points for the OECD Guidelines on Multinational Enterprises on the Rana Plaza tragedy, 25 June 2013, and follow-up statement 'One Year after Rana Plaza' 25 June 2014, on www.mneguidelines.oecd.org ; and French National Contact Point, NCP Report on Implementation of the OECD Guidelines in the Textile and Clothing Sector, 2 December 2013. The latter report lists 10 recommendations to enterprises, from 1) formalising ethical commitments, to 10) participating in compensation and reparation for damage when a direct link is established.

Chapter 4. The Labour Relations Content of the Guidelines

118. Chapter V on employment and industrial relations contains eight separate Guidelines. These are further explained in a commentary twice the length of the main text. Further explanations are provided by some of the clarifications of the original 1976 text issued by the CIME – although a number of these were incorporated in the commentary during the 2000 revision, while others have been overtaken by economic developments.

119. Enterprises are expected to live up to the Employment and Industrial Relations Guidelines 'within the framework of applicable law, regulations and prevailing labour relations and employment practices and applicable international standards'. This so-called 'chapeau' of the chapter underlines that MNEs, while operating within the jurisdiction of particular countries, may be subject to national, sub-national as well as supra-national levels of regulation. As noted further above, the reference to 'the framework of applicable law' does not exclude that the Guidelines represent supplementary standards of behaviour.

§1. Core Labour Standards

120. The first paragraph of this chapter captures the four fundamental principles and labour rights from the ILO's 1998 Declaration on Fundamental Principles and Rights at Work, namely the freedom of association and right to collective bargaining, the effective abolition of child labour, the elimination of all forms of forced or compulsory labour, and non-discrimination in employment and occupation. These principles and rights have been developed in more detailed ILO Conventions and Recommendations which are referred to in the commentary to the paragraph. Of the four items, child labour and forced labour had not been contained in the original 1976 text.

121. The commentary also notes that the ILO is the competent body to set and deal with international labour standards – an acknowledgement of the language agreed during the 1996 WTO meeting in Singapore. It also confirms the parallel nature between the OECD Guidelines and the ILO's 1977 (last revised in 2006) Tripartite Declaration of Principles on Multinational Enterprises and Social Policy as concerns employment, training, working conditions and industrial relations (although in contrast to the ILO Declaration, the OECD Guidelines cover all major aspects of corporate behaviour).

122. In fact, the textual changes made to the Employment and Industrial Relations chapter during the 2011 update show, much more than was the case during previous revisions, the will of the negotiating parties in the OECD Investment Committee to align the Guidelines recommendations with the principles expressed in the ILO Tripartite Declaration. Reference is now made in the OECD text to a large number of ILO Conventions and Recommendations. This alignment goes all the way to certain details in terminology; for example, text on 'employees of MNEs' in previous versions was replaced by the terms 'workers employed by MNEs' or 'workers in their employment', corresponding to the usage in the ILO Tripartite Declaration and, more fundamentally, to the many dimensions that employment relationships have developed in modern economies characterized by the growth of fixed-term arrangements, temporary agency work and subcontracting relationships.

123. The commentary to Chapter V recommends to enterprises to let themselves be guided, when determining the existence of an employment relationship, by the list of indicators laid out in ILO Recommendation 198 of 2006 on the employment relationship, paragraphs 13 a and b. It is understood that the definition of an employment relationship goes much beyond the status of an employee on the direct payroll of the company. By contrast, it can encompass many forms of 'disguised' employment practices which the commentary sees as occurring when 'an employer treats an individual as other than an employee in a manner that hides his or her true legal status'.[30]

I. Freedom of Association and Right to Collective Bargaining

124. Paragraph 1a obliges enterprises 'to respect the right of workers employed by the multinational enterprise to establish or join trade unions and representative organizations of their own choosing'. This wording corresponds to the provisions laid down in ILO Convention 87 on the Right to organize, which is meant to guarantee the legitimate right of trade unions as well as other types of representatives to represent the interests of the company workforce. As the CIME pointed out in clarifications as early as the 1980s, the thrust of this Guidelines provision is towards having management adopt a positive approach towards the activities of trade unions and other *bona fide* representatives of employees of all categories and in particular, an open attitude towards organizational activities (the *bona fide* language was dropped in the 2011 update).[31]

---

30. Further guidance is given in the ILO document *The Employment Relationship: An Annotated Guide to ILO Recommendation No. 198,* of May 2007, http://www.ilo.org/ifpdial/areas-of-work/labour-law/WCMS_172417/lang – en/index.htm.
    The Recommendation itself lists the following possible indicators:
    (a) the fact that the work: is carried out according to the instructions and under the control of another party; involves the integration of the worker in the organization of the enterprise; is performed solely or mainly for the benefit of another person; must be carried out personally by the worker; is carried out within specific working hours or at a workplace specified or agreed by the party requesting the work; is of a particular duration and has a certain continuity; requires the worker's availability; or involves the provision of tools, materials and machinery by the party requesting the work;
    (b) periodic payment of remuneration to the worker; the fact that such remuneration constitutes the worker's sole or principal source of income; provision of payment in kind, such as food, lodging or transport; recognition of entitlements such as weekly rest and annual holidays; payment by the party requesting the work for travel undertaken by the worker in order to carry out the work; or absence of financial risk for the worker.
31. Clarifying its position concerning 'union busting' activities, the CIME Committee condemned in its 1984 Review Report the 'active efforts [which] have been undertaken to discourage organizing

125. The Guidelines text is silent about which type of organizations or employee representatives should be engaging in collective bargaining or what criteria should be used for their recognition. Of interest in this context are the views expressed by the CIME in early clarifications as to whether international trade secretariats (ITS) could act as representative organizations.[32] The international trade secretariats and TUAC claimed at the time that the ITS are trade unions, and should be recognized by the MNEs on the basis of paragraph 1 of the Employment and Industrial Relations chapter. One case raised was that of a Dutch multinational which had allegedly refused to grant permission for leave of absence for participation at an international trade union seminar on developments within the company. The employer's view was that local law and practice should prevail, that labour relations systems were national and not international, and that there was no reason why, given this state of affairs, he should be required to deal with an ITS for consultation or collective bargaining purposes.

126. In response, the CIME noted in a rather roundabout way that the Employment and Industrial Relations Guidelines would not 'put obstacles in the way of recognition by the management of an MNE, in agreement with the national trade unions it has recognized and consistent with national laws and practices, of an International Trade Secretariat as a 'bona fide organization of employees' referred to in paragraph 1'. The Committee added that MNE management should adopt a cooperative attitude towards the participation of employee representatives in international meetings for consultation and exchange of views.[33] The issue has not come up again since then, and one may argue that, at least in Europe, these particular statements have been overtaken by events, in particular the European Works Council Directive. Of course, fundamental disagreements persist, not only between employers and trade unions but between governments as well, on the role of international trade union action, especially concerning international collective bargaining.

127. Paragraph 1b indicates that MNEs should recognize the trade unions and representative organizations chosen by their workers for the purpose of collective bargaining and 'engage in constructive negotiations, either individually or through employers' associations, with [worker] representatives with a view to reaching agreements on terms and conditions of employment'.[34] Thus, the text takes account

---

activities by employees'. The language on a 'positive approach' and an 'open attitude' implies that employers should not interfere with the right of employees to organize. Militant anti-union attitudes and policies are seen as contrary to this approach. This does not remove an employer's right to express his opinion on trade union representation; however, there should be no anti-union campaigns or threats.(see OECD, *The OECD Guidelines for Multinational Enterprises*, Paris 1986, p. 38f).

32. The ITS have since been renamed global union federations.
33. CIME, *1979 Review Report*; *see* OECD, *The OECD Guidelines for Multinational Enterprises*, Paris 1986, p. 31f.
34. Interestingly, there is no text or Commentary on the right to strike and the settlement of industrial disputes. However, the reference to the relevant ILO Conventions recognized as fundamental must be interpreted as including Convention 98 on the Right to Organize and Collective Bargaining which includes the right to strike.

of the various possible forms of bargaining (sectoral, enterprise-based) and of their main purpose to determine wages and working conditions.[35] In further support for the collective bargaining function, paragraph 2 obliges MNEs to:

(a) provide such facilities to workers' representatives as may be necessary to assist in the development of effective collective agreements;
(b) provide information to workers' representatives which is needed for meaningful negotiations on conditions of employment.

128. As a further specification of the information requirement, paragraph 2c asks companies to 'provide information to workers and their representatives which enables them to obtain a true and fair view of the performance of the entity or, where appropriate, the enterprise as a whole'. The commentary to this paragraph gives more detail to the provision by defining such information as relating to 'the structure of the enterprise, its economic and financial situation and prospects, employment trends, and expected substantial changes in operations, taking into account legitimate requirements of business confidentiality'.[36]

129. The above text on information requirements stems from the 2000 update, when the Investment Committee in fact took up the gist of previous clarifications. For example, while the Disclosure Guideline (Chapter III) addresses the provision of information to the general public, the Investment Committee has considered that employees of MNEs may need and should have access to more specific information, beyond that available to the general public, and in a form suitable for their interests and purposes.

130. The laws, regulations and practices in member countries with respect to the provision of information by enterprises to workers and their representatives differ considerably. In some countries, statutory provisions are very extensive and detailed, whereas in others, management and labour representatives define the information which management is expected to provide on a 'good faith basis'. Against this background, this particular Guidelines provision can again be considered as setting a standard supplementary to national labour relations systems and as recommending additional rules.

35. In 1976, paragraph 1 referred to 'constructive negotiations', while paragraph 2 referred to 'effective collective agreements'. In the negotiations leading up to the 2000 revision, a proposal by Australia, seconded by New Zealand, to add 'individual' to 'collective' agreements was rejected.

36. This list of items is similar to that contained in the European Works Council Directive, which nevertheless adds, *inter alia*, 'the situation and probable trend of investment' and 'the introduction of new working methods and production processes'. The Guidelines commentary adds the caveat that 'considerations of business confidentiality may mean that information on certain points may not be provided, or may not be provided without safeguards'.

II. Abolition of Child Labour and Elimination of Forced or Compulsory Labour

131. These two labour standards were introduced to the Guidelines during the 2000 revision. Child labour and forced/compulsory labour are presented in two different sub-paragraphs, first to echo the treatment of the two issues in the 1998 ILO Declaration on Fundamental Principles and Rights at Work, and second, to better enable varying language referring to each of them. The recommendation that enterprises 'contribute to' the abolition/elimination of child and forced labour is used to indicate that companies should co-operate in goals that nonetheless remain a primary responsibility of governments.

132. Paragraph 1c urges enterprises to contribute to the effective abolition of child labour, using the words of the 1998 ILO Declaration; however, it continues by saying, in reference to ILO Convention 182 concerning the worst forms of child labour, that they should 'take immediate and effective measures to secure the prohibition and elimination of the worst forms of child labour as a matter of urgency'. The Commentary makes reference to Convention 138 and Recommendation 146 (both adopted in 1973) concerning minimum ages for admission to employment as long-standing ILO instruments on child labour. It also draws attention to the linkages between poverty and child labour and to the role MNEs can – and should – play in helping to address the root causes of poverty and thus contributing to lasting solutions to the problem of child labour. Behind this language is the concern that in certain areas of the world the deprivation of any employment could lead to even worse hardship for children as well as their families. Examples of positive contributions by enterprises include ensuring that children who work are given the opportunity to attend school.[37]

133. The ILO has estimated that currently over 20 million people are victims of forced labour, with migrants being the largest single group of victims. Guidelines paragraph 1(d) recommends that enterprises contribute to the elimination of all forms of compulsory labour, another principle derived from the 1998 ILO Declaration. The reference to this core labour right is based on the ILO Conventions 29 of 1930 and 105 of 1957 which both, in different wording, oblige ratifying countries to terminate the use of forced and compulsory labour in all its forms. Correspondingly, a textual addition in the 2011 update asks enterprises to 'take adequate steps to ensure that forced or compulsory labour does not exist in their operations'. Negotiators during the 2000 update were aware of the difficult issue of regulating prison labour in view of these Conventions. On this issue, they agreed on pointing out in the commentary that the ILO is the competent body to deal with prison labour, in particular as concerns the 'hiring-out of prisoners to (or their placing at the disposal of) private individuals, companies or associations'.

37. The corresponding text in the commentary was added upon the recommendation of the Brazilian delegation.

III. Equal Employment Opportunity and the Principle of Non-discrimination

134. Paragraph 1e on non-discrimination goes beyond a (negative) list of discriminatory factors by asking enterprises to apply the 'principle of equality of opportunity and treatment in employment' throughout their operations. The list of non-permissible grounds for discrimination with respect to employment or occupation (race, colour, sex, religion, political opinion, national extraction, social origin) is taken from ILO Convention 111 of 1958, which considers that any distinction, exclusion or preference on these grounds is in violation of the Convention. The list also includes discrimination for 'other status' which, as noted in the Commentary, refers to trade union activity and personal characteristics such as age, disability, pregnancy, marital status, sexual orientation or HIV status. The commentary also points out that the principle of non-discrimination is considered to apply to such terms and conditions as hiring, job assignment, discharge, pay and benefits, promotion, transfer or relocation, termination, training and retirement.

135. With respect to pay, no effort is made to further define equal pay (such as in 'equal pay for work of equal value'). A reference to equal employment opportunity (including 'positive discrimination') policies was retained from the original 1976 text, i.e. enterprises are expected to promote equal opportunities for women and men with special emphasis on selection, remuneration, and promotion.

§2. Consultation and Cooperation

136. The 2000 update introduced a reference to consultation ('Enterprises should … promote consultation and cooperation between employers and employees and their representatives on matters of mutual concern'). In 2011 the reference to 'employees' was replaced by 'workers', corresponding to the intended alignment of terminology with the 1977 ILO MNE Declaration. At the same time, the consultation clause was moved from paragraph 2c to paragraph 3 of the chapter. This reference to consultative forms of employee participation is taken from ILO Recommendation 94 concerning Consultation and Cooperation between Employers and Workers at the Level of the Undertaking. It also conforms to a provision contained in the 1977 ILO Declaration. The commentary is right to point out that such consultative arrangements should not substitute for employees' right to bargain over terms and conditions of employment. Based on this addition of a reference to consultation, it can be concluded that the information requirements in paragraph 2 as outlined above (true and fair view, etc.) form the basis for both effective negotiation and consultation.

§3. Appropriate Employment and Industrial Relations Standards

137. According to paragraph 4a, MNEs should 'observe standards of employment and industrial relations not less favourable than those observed by comparable employers in the host country'. The commentary clarifies that employment and industrial relations standards are understood to include compensation and working-time arrangements. In this context, it should be noted that the Guidelines do not prevent a subsidiary of an MNE from adjusting wages in a case when it experiences economic and financial difficulties, provided that such conduct, under local law and practice, is accepted in the country for national enterprises under comparable circumstances.

138. Sections 4a and 4b are an interesting case in point for negotiated additions to the original Guidelines text. Section 4a about 'standards not less favorable than those observed by comparable employers' was included in the original 1976 Guidelines text, and the wording was subsequently adopted by the 1977 ILO MNE Declaration. However, the ILO decided to be more specific and introduce the notion of wages, noting that 'wages, benefits and conditions of work ... should not be less favourable than ...' (section 33). The OECD text subsequently remained unchanged, until the commentary in 2000 added that 'standards' as used in section 4a included compensation and working time.

139. In the 2011 update, by contrast, the notion of wages was brought directly into the text by importing a new section 4b) from the ILO MNE Declaration (section 34): 'When multinational enterprises operate in developing countries, where comparable employers may not exist, [they should] provide the best possible wages, benefits and conditions of work ... at least adequate to satisfy the basic needs of workers and their families.' Two observations may be called for: first, while the reference to standards (now explicitly including wages) in section 4a applies to all countries, the new reference to what might be called a 'living wage' in section 4b only comes up in the context of developing countries. Second, while the former section takes a 'relative' or comparative approach to the guarantee of adequate standards/wages ('not less favourable than'), the latter section introduces an 'absolute' approach (wages must be high enough to satisfy basic needs). Since commentary is missing on the latter section[38], the Guidelines user does not get full insight into why the 'absolute' approach should only apply to developing countries and the 'relative' or comparative approach to OECD and other developed countries. It remains to be seen whether cases will be brought before NCPs that touch upon this apparent lack of clarity.[39]

---

38. For example, there is no reference to the Minimum Wage Fixing Convention and Recommendation which provide most of the wording for para. 4b. There is also no definition of what constitutes 'basic needs'.
39. In fact, also in OECD countries a low wage can be insufficient to satisfy basic needs, particularly in the case of large families, and in certain countries large numbers of part-time and even full-time workers receive monthly top-ups to their wages by the welfare or social assistance administration, to bring their families up to what is considered a minimum living standard. Also, the reference to wages high enough to 'satisfy the basic needs of workers and their families' may be interpreted by some as implying that wages should depend on family size. In 2011 BIAC only agreed to this wording when TUAC confirmed that they did not intend to use this clause for demanding that wages should be dependent on family size.

140. The reference to occupational health and safety as an employment standard in paragraph 4c implies that MNEs are expected to follow prevailing regulatory standards and industry norms to minimize the risk of accidents and injury to health arising out of, linked with, or occurring in, the course of employment. This should encourage enterprises to work to raise the level of performance with respect to occupational health and safety in all parts of their operation even where this may not be formally required by existing regulations in the countries in which they operate.[40] As noted in the commentary, this text is also meant to encourage enterprises to respect workers' ability to remove themselves from a work situation when there is reasonable justification to believe that it presents an imminent and serious risk to health or safety. Health and safety concerns are echoed elsewhere in the Guidelines, most notably in the chapters on consumer interests and the environment.

§4. Employment and Training of Local Personnel

141. The recommendation in paragraph 5 of the chapter encourages MNEs to recruit an adequate workforce share locally, including managerial personnel, and to provide adequate training to them. Language in this paragraph on training and skill levels complements the text in paragraph 4 of the General Policies chapter on encouraging human capital formation. The reference to the employment of local workers complements the text encouraging local capacity building in paragraph 3 of the same chapter. The reference in the paragraph to training and skill formation being a matter for labour/management dialogue ('in co-operation with employee representatives') ought to be noted.

§5. Reasonable Notice

142. Paragraph 6 takes up an aspect relating to the security of employment; it recommends that enterprises provide reasonable notice to workers' representatives and relevant government authorities of changes in their operations which would have major effects upon the livelihood of their employees, in particular the closure of an entity involving collective layoffs or dismissals. The apparent purpose of this provision is to afford an opportunity for cooperation to mitigate the adverse effects of such changes. Reasonable notice and mitigation of adverse effects are important principles that are widely reflected in the industrial relations laws and practices of adhering countries, although the approaches taken to ensuring an opportunity for meaningful cooperation vary considerably. Mitigation of adverse effects would usually include looking for alternative solutions to immediate dismissal (such as retraining, work sharing, restrictions to overtime, etc.)

40. This expectation expressed in the commentary is in line with the 'precautionary principle' in the environment chapter of the Guidelines which notes that enterprises should 'not use the lack of full scientific certainty as a reason for postponing cost-effective measures to prevent or minimise [environmental] damage', including that to human health and safety.

143. Alleged violations of the reasonable notice provision have been behind a number of cases brought to the CIME for clarification in the 1980s and 1990s, and to NCPs since then. One CIME clarification from the 1980s stated that 'it would conform to the general intention of this paragraph ... if management were able to give such notice prior to the final decision being taken', and the negotiators of the 2000 update decided to bring this clarification into the main text of the Guidelines. Indeed, notice prior to the final decision is a feature of industrial relations laws and practices in a number of adhering countries. Upon the proposal of the US delegation, however, a last-minute proviso was included in the text in 2000, to the effect that 'other means may also be employed to provide meaningful co-operation to mitigate the effects of such decisions'.[41]

§6. Unfair Influence in *Bona fide* Negotiations

144. Following paragraph 7 enterprises should:

> in the context of bona fide negotiations with workers' representatives on conditions of employment, or while workers are exercising a right to organize, not threaten to transfer the whole or part of an operating unit from the country concerned nor transfer workers from the enterprises' component entities in other countries in order to influence unfairly those negotiations or to hinder the exercise of a right to organize.

This paragraph takes up two interrelated issues referring to company policy when confronted with union formation, union negotiation or industrial disputes: in response to such action, companies are asked (i) not to transfer, or threaten to transfer, an establishment or parts thereof; and (ii) not to import personnel from outside the country.

145. On the former item, would a warning from management that certain employee or trade union demands, and the costs they entail for the firm, might negatively influence future investment decisions, or even lead to disinvestment, be a violation of the Guidelines? The CIME has clarified that a distinction should be made between information given to employees during negotiations on the likely consequences of certain demands for the viability of the firm which is legitimately provided by management, on the one hand, and threats which would be an unfair use of management's negotiating power, on the other. 'Unfair' is the key notion in this context – a concept which, particularly in the United Sates, indicates employer conduct that tends to coerce employees, not only through physical violence or the threat thereof, but through more subtle means of coercion as well.

41. The CIME had considered earlier that the sensitivity of certain business decisions and the potential for serious damage to an enterprise may make it difficult for management, when considering major changes in activities, to give employee representatives early notice of such changes. However, such considerations would only apply in exceptional circumstances.

146. Obviously it is difficult to distinguish between a threat and a mere statement of information designed to guide employees in reaching an un-coerced conclusion. Considering the right to freedom of expression, the expression of opinions or information by management can certainly not be prohibited. However, the US National Labour Relations Board has considered certain threatening statements as evidence of 'bad faith' bargaining.[42]

147. The latter clause on the import of personnel was added to the original Guidelines text after the *Hertz* case in the late 1970s, where Hertz Rental Car transferred workers from branches in southern Sweden to replace Danish workers on strike. This practice led to agreement among all parties that such use of strike breakers in the sense of a transfer of workers from foreign affiliates in order to influence negotiations or hinder the right to organize, although not covered by the 1976 Guidelines text, was not to be tolerated. This gap was filled through an amendment, which was in line with the ILO MNE Declaration, and also with the regulations on the freedom of movement of workers in the EU. For example, the European Council of Ministers has issued an opinion to the effect that the free movement of labour within the countries of the European Union was only to be used in the positive sense of contributing to the well-being and promotion of workers.[43]

148. Consequently, transfer of workers from one foreign affiliate to another, as strike breakers or otherwise to unfairly influence bargaining, is also covered by paragraph 7. The 1977 ILO MNE Declaration had already done so by including the stipulation in paragraph 52 (now 53) 'nor should they transfer workers from affiliates in foreign countries with a view to undermining *bona fide* negotiations with the workers' representatives or the workers' exercise of the right to organize'.

---

42. A. L. Goldman and R. L. Corrada, *Labour Law and Industrial Relations in the United States of America* (2010). In 2003, a case on these grounds was brought before the Swiss NCP by trade unions complaining against an operating unit of Nestle in South Korea.
43. Article 48 of the Treaty establishing the European Economic Community (treaty of Rome) reads as follows:

    1. Freedom of movement of workers shall be ensured within the Community …
    2. Such freedom … shall entail the abolition of any discrimination based on nationality between workers of the Member States as regards employment, remuneration, and other conditions of work and employment.
    3. It shall include the right:
        a. To accept offers of employment actually made.
        b. To move about freely within the territory of Member States for this purpose;
        c. To stay in a Member State for the purpose of employment in conformity with the provisions governing the employment of nationals of that State laid down by law, regulation or administrative action;
        d. To remain in the territory of a Member State after having been employed in that state …

149. Obviously, cross-border transfer of workers in a case of conflict is not a frequent phenomenon, given the difficulties of obtaining work permits and the like, except perhaps in common markets, like the EU, where there is freedom of labour movement. It should be added that transfer of workers from one subsidiary to another within the same country does not seem, in the actual status of the text and Commentary, to be covered by the Guideline.

150. The Guideline may be considered limited in other respects, as well. As it refers to threats to transfer the whole or a part of an operating unit from the country concerned, it covers only existing plants and equipment. Threats not to engage in future investment are not covered. Neither does the text refer to the transfer of products or materials, nor to the fact that certain subsidiaries may be doing 'overtime' work to compensate for pending strikes in other locations. Thus, the Guidelines do not seem to provide an angle for bringing complaints against company practices, often deplored by trade unions, to set productivity performance of one establishment against another, with the (tacit or not) understanding that the less productive units may suffer from disinvestment.

§7. Access to the Real Decision-makers

151. Paragraph 8 recommends that MNEs 'enable authorized representatives of the workers in their employment to negotiate on collective bargaining or labour–management relations issues and allow the parties to consult on matters of mutual concern with representatives of management who are authorized to take decisions on these matters'. This Guideline covers the issue of access to the real decision-makers in the company. The issue is one that goes to the heart of the multinational matter. The decision-making structure of a multinational enterprise and its parent-subsidiary relationships may indeed have the consequence that the subsidiary is not fully empowered to negotiate and conclude agreements and that strategic decisions affecting the livelihood of the employees are taken in far-away head offices, with the possibility that even local managers are only informed *ex post* about decisions which affect the subsidiary they manage.

152. The Guidelines are clear on this point: there must be timely information and access to real decision makers during negotiation and consultation. While timely information is also prescribed by paragraph 6 of the chapter, it is also self-evident that a parent company must provide local management with appropriate authority and sufficient information so that they can take decisions on matters under negotiation, unless top management itself prefers to negotiate directly, sending duly authorized representatives from headquarters for such negotiations. In 1980 the CIME gave a clarification to this effect at the occasion of the Viggo-British Oxygen case, where workers' representatives at the Viggo subsidiary (Sweden) had allegedly not been able to negotiate with the real decision-makers on future investment policies of the company.

153. The key terms used in this paragraph still date from the original 1976 Guidelines text; however, a reference to 'consultation' has been added since, following the text in paragraph 3. Thus, both the terms 'negotiation' and 'consultation' are now used throughout the chapter. The Committee has observed (1982 Review Report) that in industrial relations generally the distinction between the two concepts is difficult to draw in practice. As a general rule, the concept of negotiation implies an effort to reach agreement by the parties concerned. In some national systems, the term negotiation, as distinct from consultation, means that if in case of disagreement a party takes a unilateral decision, the other party is justified in having recourse to industrial action or to external decision-making procedures (conciliation, arbitration, courts). 'Consultation' is often used to denote situations where management retains a right to make and to carry out the decision it thinks best, having listened to the views of employee representatives. In some cases consultations may also be understood to imply an effort to reach agreement, although the final decision-making power of management remains unaffected.

154. The addition in paragraph 1 of the term 'collective bargaining' in 2011 has further clarified the Guidelines, since it is understood that the terminology is aligned with ILO usage and, in particular, Convention 98. When considering the language in paragraph 8 about negotiations 'on collective bargaining or labour-management relations issues', it needs to be kept in mind that there is wide diversity among adhering countries concerning national practices with respect to both of these. While in some countries, collective bargaining or labour-management relations are limited to more traditional conditions of employment, such as wages, working hours, and health and safety standards, in other countries, there is a trend towards including information and consultation on the economic and financial management of the enterprise, extending even to future production and investment plans. As they are used in the Guidelines, the terms are sufficiently broad to permit a variety of interpretations in light of different national situations.

§8. The Use of National Languages

155. The issue has been raised concerning the use of national language in negotiations, consultations, cooperation and the provision of information by MNEs to employee representatives. In fact, a number of paragraphs of the Guidelines on Employment and Industrial Relations are of direct relevance. Negotiations, consultations, cooperation or provision of information imply effective communication between the parties concerned. As a general rule, it is expected that management and worker representatives will communicate in a language effectively understood by both. There may, however, be cases, for example meetings where representatives from the parent company and a certain number of worker representatives from multiple countries are involved, where there is no common language understood by all. In such cases the CIME has judged that adequate interpreter and translation facilities should be provided (1984 Review Report). Since that time, the number of global works councils and world company councils has multiplied, but MNE management usually makes sure that adequate translation is provided, so that no serious complaints of local representatives about lack of comprehension have been heard of in recent years.[44]

44. For a discussion of principal features of global works and company councils, see Stefan Rüb, *World Works Councils and Other Forms of Global Employee Representation in Transnational Undertakings*, 2002.

Chapter 5. The Implementation of the Guidelines

§1. Introduction

156. On top of modifying the substantive text, the 2000 review of the OECD Guidelines substantially changed their implementation procedures which had initially been decided by the OECD Council in 1976, the main new feature being the strengthening of the NCPs. The 2011 update introduced further substantive improvements, in particular of the structure and processes of NCPs. In fact, to many critics improving and strengthening the Guidelines' implementation procedures in the sense of 'giving them more teeth'– is at least as important as textual changes. In fact, these 'teeth' set apart the OECD Guidelines from other international instruments which lack an effective implementation or grievance mechanism. The availability of such grievance mechanisms can contribute to improving access to remedy for victims of violations of rights or principles under the Guidelines, even though NCPs are no judicial bodies and remedy may sometimes be limited or even impossible.

157. The Guidelines' current implementation procedures are laid down, first, in the June 2011 Council Decision on Implementation Procedures which outlines the responsibilities of both the Investment Committee and NCPs; second, in the Procedural Guidance given both actors by the Investment Committee; and third in further detailed commentary on all of the above. Since the 2000 update, the NCPs are in the forefront as the key government institution responsible for promoting effective implementation of the Guidelines. In addition to promotional activities, NCPs handle enquiries on the Guidelines, and act as mediators and problem-solvers in 'specific instances', i.e. when complaints or requests for clarifying certain provisions are raised. Before 2000, such cases usually bypassed the NCPs, and were submitted directly to the Committee for clarification.

158. The Council Decisions of 2000 and 2011 have provided detailed guidance to NCPs in fulfilling their role. The 2000 Decision included (a) clarification of the roles and responsibilities of the NCPs by means of a new text on procedural guidance; (b) the holding of annual meetings involving all NCPs, to allow them to share their experiences in promoting the Guidelines and handling individual cases; and (c) the requirement for each of them to submit an annual report of its activities to the OECD Investment Committee.[45]

159. The additional revisions in 2011 included (a) an emphasis on making the results of proceedings publicly available; (b) indicative timeframes for NCP procedures; (c) fostering functional equivalence among NCPs, *inter alia* through peer reviews; (d) stronger guidance on coordination between NCPs in handling specific instances; and (e) a new approach to the issue of parallel proceedings.

---

45. See the most recent coordinates of NCPs at http://www.oecd.org/daf/inv/mne/ncps.htm.

160. The 2011 Review has also clarified once again the INV Committee's oversight role. The Committee is expected to continue to provide clarifications of the meaning of the Guidelines and is encouraged to pursue a proactive agenda that promotes the effective observance by enterprises of Guidelines standards.

161. Finally, with regard to non-adhering countries, the Guidelines make clear that the recommendations represent good practice wherever enterprises operate, not just within the OECD area. Nevertheless, implementation procedures will naturally be different in non-adhering countries (for example, there are no NCPs to handle individual cases). Importantly, since the 2000 Review, a majority of the issues raised have referred to corporate conduct in non-adhering countries.

§2. Institutional Mechanisms

162. The institutional set-up for promoting and implementing the Guidelines is outlined in the June 2011 OECD Council Decision and its accompanying Procedural Guidance. It consists of three main elements: the NCPs; the Investment Committee; and the advisory committees to the OECD of business and labour federations, the Business and Industry Advisory Committee (BIAC) and the Trade Union Advisory Committee (TUAC), respectively. Starting with the 2011 update, OECD Watch is now recognized as an advisory party on an equal footing with BIAC and TUAC. Other international partners are also invited for collaboration.

163. The NCPs are responsible for encouraging observance of the Guidelines in their national context and for ensuring that the Guidelines are well known and understood by the national business community and by other interested parties. Already in its 1979 Review Report, and again in the 1984 review, the CIME asked member countries which had not already done so to provide facilities for handling enquiries and for discussions with the parties concerned on matters related to the Guidelines. The Committee considered that, as a general principle, such prior contacts and discussions at the national level should take place before matters are raised directly at Committee level. Setting up these contact points was seen as helping to encourage responsible business conduct and minimize violations of labour, environmental and other standards as a result of MNE activities. Nevertheless, although many countries subsequently established contact points, they largely remained non-operational throughout the 1980s and 1990s, and complaints or requests for clarification were usually directly addressed to the Committee. By contrast, in early 2016, with one or two exceptions among recent adherents, all adhering governments have an NCP in place to handle enquiries and complaints.

164. In sum, NCPs are supposed to:

- handle enquiries about the Guidelines;
- assist in solving problems related to the observance of Guidelines standards by means of conciliation and mediation, thus providing access to remedy (see the section 'Implementation in Specific Instances' below);

– undertake promotional activities and inform interested parties about the availability of their facilities;
– gather information on national experiences with the Guidelines, share them during regular meetings, and report about them to the Investment Committee.

165. The effectiveness of the NCP is a crucial factor in determining how influential the Guidelines are in each national context. While it is recognized that governments should be accorded flexibility in the way they organize NCPs – they 'can use different forms of organization … to meet their objectives'– 'functional equivalence' is nevertheless expected and all NCPs are asked to follow four core criteria in carrying out their activities: visibility, accessibility, transparency and accountability. For example, easy access to NCPs by national stakeholders is essential for their effective functioning. The accountability of NCPs is enhanced by a provision calling for annual reports of their activity, which serve as a basis for exchanges of view among the adhering governments. As a rule, the reports contain information on the nature and results of NCP activities, including problem-solving activities in specific instances. As to the criterion of transparency, conflicts with the need for confidentiality of proceedings may arise (to be discussed further below). To ensure NCP effectiveness, the OECD Council also requests countries to make available to them the necessary human and financial resources, and to enable them to cooperate with each other as necessary.[46]

166. NCPs provide the OECD annually with information on their organizational structures. In early 2016, the NCPs in 42 OECD and other adhering countries were structured as follows:

– monoagency: the NCP is composed of one or more representatives of a single ministry (for example Argentina, Ireland and Poland);
– monoagency 'plus': the NCP secretariat is located in one ministry, but other ministries or stakeholders are involved in the work of the NCP on an advisory basis (for example Australia, Italy and the United States);
– interagency: the NCP is composed of representatives of two or more ministries (for example Brazil, Germany and the United Kingdom).
– tripartite: the NCP is composed of representatives of one or more ministries, business associations, and trade unions (for example Belgium, France and Sweden);
– quadripartite: the NCP is composed of representatives of one or more ministries, business associations, trade unions, and NGOs (Czech Republic and Finland);
– independent agency: the NCP is generally composed of independent experts connected to a ministry and usually benefiting from Secretariat staff within the ministry (Denmark, the Netherlands and Norway).[47]

46. The NCPs' endowment with resources to enable them to discharge their functions remains uneven. Only about a third have a dedicated budget, and most of them have only one to three staff members, often part-time (*Annual Report on the OECD Guidelines for Multinational Enterprises 2014*, pp. 22f; OECD document DAF/INV/NCP(2015)1)
47. OECD, *Annual Report on the OECD Guidelines for Multinational Enterprises 2015* (Paris, 2016).

167. NCPs also report the existence of other means for organizing consultations and liaising with other stakeholders. For example, a number of countries with 'government-only' NCPs report the use of advisory committees whose members include non-government partners. Others state that they convene regular meetings with business, trade unions and civil society. Still others state that they have had consultations with NGOs or other stakeholders on an informal basis or in reference to specific issues where the latter's specific expertise is required. Such activities are in conformity with the Commentary on the implementation procedures which states that 'NCPs, whatever their composition, are expected to develop and maintain relations with representatives of the business community, worker organizations, other non-governmental organizations and other interested parties'.

168. The Investment Committee is the OECD body responsible for overseeing the functioning of the Guidelines and is expected to take steps to enhance their effectiveness. This responsibility applies not only to the Guidelines, but to all elements of the Declaration on International Investment and Multinational Enterprises. Regarding the Guidelines, the Committee's responsibilities include:

- organizing exchanges of views on matters relating to the Guidelines with social partners, NGOs and non-adhering countries;
- issuing 'clarifications' as necessary;
- reviewing the Guidelines text and NCPs' implementation practices so as to ensure the Guidelines' relevance and effectiveness;
- actively promoting the diffusion and effective observance by enterprises of the Guidelines' standards and principles;
- reporting to the OECD Council on the experience with the Guidelines.

169. Since the Guidelines continue to be of a non-binding nature, the INV Committee will not act as a judicial or quasi-judicial body. It will consider requests from NCPs for assistance, including in the event of doubt about particular Guidelines provisions, and may intervene in case of substantiated submissions that a particular NCP is not fulfilling its procedural responsibilities. However, as a rule the findings or statements made by an NCP should not be questioned through a direct referral to the Committee. In fact, the OECD Council has made it clear that an issue should come up for clarification only when 'an adhering country, an advisory body or OECD Watch makes a substantiated submission on whether an NCP has correctly interpreted the Guidelines in specific instances'. Even when the Committee accepts a case for clarification, it shall not reach conclusions on the conduct of individual enterprises. This provision is in contrast to the principle that final statements by NCPs on the results of their mediation efforts in specific instances should normally be transparent and include the names of the conflicting parties.[48] Even in the case of clarifications that avoid naming the enterprise in question, however, it has never been difficult in the past for outside observers to find out the details of the case.

48. See the publicly available information on all cases in the OECD's specific instances database, available on-line, http://mneguidelines.oecd.org/.

170. As the Guidelines are addressed to enterprises, business and labour input is especially important. The Committee regularly consults with BIAC and TUAC on matters relating to the Guidelines and on other issues concerning international investment and MNEs. As outlined in Chapter 1 of this monograph, BIAC and TUAC are accredited to the OECD as official advisory bodies.

171. The two advisory bodies may request consultations with the NCPs on issues related to the Guidelines. BIAC and TUAC can also raise such issues directly with the Committee. In addition, they are meant to inform their member federations about developments in the Guidelines and to seek their members' inputs in Guidelines implementation procedures. They also participate in promotional activities organized by NCPs or OECD bodies on a national, regional or multilateral basis.

172. Non-governmental organizations (NGOs) were first involved in the 2000 Guidelines review. With their clearinghouse OECD Watch, they were a major player in the 2011 update. They may request consultations with the NCPs on issues related to Guidelines; they can also participate in promotional activities organized by the NCPs or by the Committee, and actually organize such activities themselves. As already outlined in Chapter 1, OECD Watch is now considered an 'accredited stakeholder' and participates regularly in consultations with the INV Committee.

§3. Promoting and Implementing the Guidelines

173. The OECD Council Decision on Implementation Procedures and the Procedural Guidance describe the various manners by which the governments of adhering countries have agreed to promote the implementation of the Guidelines by enterprises operating in or from their territory.

I. Information and Promotion

174. Although the Committee itself may organize promotional activities like symposia, seminars or other conferences, information and promotion of the Guidelines is essentially the role of NCPs. The Council Decision requires NCPs to make the Guidelines better known and available by appropriate means, including through on-line information and in national languages. In addition to 18 language versions available on the OECD website, many NCPs not covered by the OECD's own translations have taken the initiative to publish the Guidelines text and commentary online through their NCP website.[49] In their efforts to raise awareness of the Guidelines and promote corporate social responsibility, NCPs cooperate with a wide variety of organizations and individuals, including the business community, trade unions and other NGOs.

49. The 'official' OECD language versions remain in English and French. Trade unions from the Russian Federation have also translated the Guidelines into Russian.

175. Targeted workshops, or brochures explaining how to file complaints before an NCP, can be important tools. As a rule, NCPs also tend to provide prospective investors, both inward and outward, with information about the Guidelines. High-level promotion has included references to the Guidelines in statements coming out of G7/G8 summits and Finance Ministers' meetings.[50] However, the OECD Secretariat remains critical of the fact that only a minority of NCPs regularly produce annual reports available on line and that only half of them distribute brochures or have developed any notable promotional plan.

176. To varying degrees, adhering governments have expressed their support for the Guidelines through other aspects of national policy. Many governments make efforts to call attention to the Guidelines among foreign investors or domestic exporters, in particular by referring to them in various ways in the context of export credit and/or international investment promotion or guarantee programmes.[51] Almost all adhering countries have set up such linkages. For example, in France, companies applying for export credits or investment guarantees are systematically informed about the Guidelines. This information takes the form of a letter from the organization in charge of managing such programmes as well as a paper for companies to sign acknowledging that they have 'read and understood the OECD Guidelines'. Furthermore, in the Netherlands applicants for such programmes or facilities receive copies of the Guidelines and, in order to qualify, must state that they are aware of the Guidelines and that they will endeavour to comply with them to the best of their ability. MNEs in Germany face similar requirements. While TUAC endorses such linkages between export credits and MNEs' endorsement of the Guidelines, BIAC representatives have warned that this might change their long-established voluntary and non-binding character.

177. By contrast, the Guidelines do not ask MNEs themselves to publicly report their adherence. In the past, the CIME had, for example, recommended 'to all enterprises concerned that they indicate publicly their acceptance of the Guidelines', preferably in their annual reports (CIME 1979 and 1984 Review Reports), but this no longer seems to be a priority for the Committee.

---

50. For example, at the 2003 G8 summit at Evian heads of state and government welcomed 'voluntary initiatives by companies that promote corporate social and environmental responsibility, such as the OECD Guidelines for Multinational Enterprises'; in the 2007 G8 Summit Declaration at Heiligendamm/Germany, leaders committed themselves to 'promote actively internationally agreed corporate social responsibility and labour standards (such as the OECD Guidelines for Multinational Enterprises and the ILO Tripartite Declaration)'; and in their 2015 statement, G7 leaders committed to strengthening 'mechanisms for providing access to remedies, including the National Contact Points'.

51. This is in line with the Recommendation of the Council on Common Approaches for Officially Supported Export Credits and Environmental and Social Due Diligence, as adopted by the OECD Council on 28 June 2012: see OECD document TAD/ECG(2012)5. See also OECD, Annual Report on the OECD Guidelines for Multinational Enterprises 2014, Annex Table 1.A3, pp. 83ff., for more detail about the various forms this linkage takes in adhering countries.

II. Implementation in Specific Instances

178. The specific instance mechanism is a unique feature of NCPs, distinguishing the Guidelines from other international instruments in the area of responsible business conduct. In principle, any interested party or organization may approach an NCP to enquire about a matter related to the Guidelines. When issues arise concerning implementation of the Guidelines in relation to specific business conduct (usually based on complaints by trade unions or NGOs), the NCP is expected to help resolve them. Generally, issues are dealt with by the NCP in whose country the issue has arisen, but depending on the type of parent–subsidiary relationship further contacts at the bilateral or even trilateral level may be pursued between separate NCPs in adhering countries; in particular, the text on implementation procedures asks that 'the NCP of the host country should consult with the NCP of the home country'. As guiding principles for their handling of specific instances, NCPs should act in an *impartial, predictable* and *equitable* manner.

179. Impartiality of NCP proceedings in the resolution of complaints is of particular importance. This implies that NCPs should not show bias towards either party to a case – a critical element of an NCP's success since impartiality and credibility are intimately linked and, taken together, will increase the likelihood that the instrument is used by potential complainants.

180. An NCP's consideration of complaints is usually composed of three phases. It will first make an initial assessment of whether the complaints or issues raised merit examination, *inter alia* by determining whether the issue is *bona fide* and substantiated. In over half of cases rejected at the initial assessment stage – 35 since the 2011 update – the respective NCP cited lack of substantiation as the cause. In the affirmative, the NCP will offer its good offices to help the parties involved to resolve the issues. It will usually consult with all parties involved and seek advice from relevant national authorities, and may subsequently offer, or facilitate access to, conciliation or mediation. This process can be significantly quicker and less costly than court proceedings and aims at mutual agreement rather than a court judgment.

181. At the conclusion of the procedures, final agreements or other results of the proceedings should, as a rule, be made publicly available. This can take the following forms:

- a statement when the NCP determines that the issue raised should not be considered further;
- a statement when no agreement is reached or when a party is unwilling to participate constructively, in which cases the Contact Point is nevertheless expected to express its views or make such recommendations for action as it considers appropriate; however, NCPs are not required to ascertain whether a company has violated the Guidelines;

– a report when the parties have reached agreement, including information on the procedures initiated by the NCP, and on the content of the agreement if the parties involved agree.

182. A Final Report may or may not include an asessment as to whether a company conduct was or was not in conformity with the standards of the OECD Guidelines. While a negative assessment may damage a company's reputation, an assessment concluding that there has been no violation of standards can protect it against further complaints.

183. Thus, transparency is recognized as a general principle for the conduct of NCPs. Nonetheless, it is generally understood that a balance needs to be struck between transparency and confidentiality in order to build confidence in the Guidelines procedures. First, in the course of the proceedings confidentiality should be maintained. Next, when drafting a public statement, 'the need to protect sensitive business and other stakeholder information' should be taken into account by the NCP – although the commentary to the Implementation Procedures clarifies once again that 'the proceedings … will normally be confidential [while] the results will normally be transparent'. While assurance of confidentiality provides incentives for parties to discuss openly and candidly the alternatives for conflict resolution, too much confidentiality can lead to a lack of sincere engagement, as non-cooperative parties do not need to fear negative publicity. It goes without saying that in practice there have been differences in emphasis on this point between the trade union and the business community.[52] The 2011 update has tried to restrict differential practices among NCPs, both in relation to disclosure of information while a case is being considered and after it has been concluded (see section C.4 of the Procedural Guidance and the respective commentary, paragraphs 31ff.).

184. NCP views have also differed on the potential impact of situations where a specific instance raised before them is also the subject of legal or administrative procedures in a given country (for example a case involving the issue of appropriate prior notice in case of plant closures). While certain countries see no problem in having such procedures in parallel, some NCPs have tended to refuse to accept specific instances already covered by legal proceedings. The 2011 Guidelines update has provided some guidance on the issue by requesting of NCPs not to 'decide that issues do not merit further consideration solely because parallel proceedings have been conducted, are under way or are available to the parties concerned'. However, the NCP needs to evaluate whether its conciliation or mediation efforts would not unduly interfere with court proceedings or even cause a 'contempt of court' situation.[53]

---

52. In particular, BIAC has been critical about naming companies in public pronouncements, while TUAC has complained that some NCPs appear to ignore the expectation to make results public and give no or little explanation to the party raising the case as to why they opt for keeping results confidential.
53. In about 20 per cent of cases not accepted after initial assessment during 2014/15, parallel proceedings were cited as the reason for non-acceptance.

185. There is, thus, not only a problem of consistency in approaches between various NCPs, but also of coordination between them. Where cases cross national boundaries, it is *per definitionem* necessary to establish good coordination across NCPs. In addition, where national laws are contradictory, NCPs need to familiarize themselves with rules and regulations in other countries. One particular example of a lack of coordination between NCPs was the case of shop closures by Marks & Spencer in several European countries in 2001/2002, where the French and Belgian contact points issued quite contradictory judgments. While the French NCP came to the conclusion that the company's notice before closure 'was not satisfactory in view of the Guidelines', the Belgian NCP, by contrast, 'did not find any violation of the Guidelines'.

186. There is no doubt that two NCPs making public contradictory evaluations of company conduct runs the risk of damaging the credibility of the implementation process, and the 2011 Guidelines update responded to this type of situation by sharpening their text on NCP coordination. Consequently, when issues arise from an enterprise's activity that takes place in several adhering countries, the NCPs involved should determine which one of them should take the lead in bringing the respective case to a solution, and also in making a final statement in the absence of an agreement.

187. Another issue concerns the engagement of the parties involved in the specific instance. In particular, some companies may not show any interest in engaging in a dialogue or may not accept the NCP as a legitimate body to deal with a complaint. Such unwillingness to cooperate can harm an NCP's capacity to act as a mediator and work for conflict resolution. While some NCPs have in the past taken the view that a case should not proceed without engagement, others have concluded that even in the face of an uncooperative party a complaint should be investigated and an assessment made as to whether an enterprise had acted in accordance with the Guidelines.[54]

188. Finally, to improve the 'functional equivalence' of NCPs and to respond to criticism about long procedural delays, a new subsection on 'Indicative Timeframe' was incorporated in the text, as revised in 2011. The new text (Commentary to Procedural Guidance, paragraphs 40–41) asks NCPs to conclude their procedures within 12 months from receipt of the specific instance. As to the various stages of the process:

- the initial assessment and decision whether to offer good offices to assist the parties should be concluded within 3 months;
- the NCP should establish a reasonable time frame for its efforts at conciliation or mediation and should critically examine whether to continue the assistance if no agreement is reached within this timeframe;

54. There are also cases of 'bad faith' engagement in the course of a complaint procedure, for example for building a case against a company outside the NCP process, through leaking documents, etc.

– a statement or report should be issued within 3 months after the conclusion of the procedure.

In contrast to these requirements, an examination of pending cases (31) on the OECD database in early 2016 shows that, for various reasons, many of them had been ongoing for over a year.

III. Clarifications

189. The 2011 update has retained the possibility of the Investment Committee issuing 'clarifications' of the meaning of the Guidelines in specific circumstances. Chapter 1 of this monograph has already listed the 35 requests for clarification submitted between 1976 and 2000. The purpose of the clarification is to provide additional information about whether and how the Guidelines apply to a particular business situation. In other words, it uses a particular case to clarify the meaning of a provision in the Guidelines and how it should be applied in future cases. Although clarifications have usually arisen in connection with the activities of a specific enterprise, they are not intended to pronounce a judgment of the appropriateness of that enterprise's conduct. In this context, it is also important to note that a substantial number of cases raised with the Investment Committee (CIME at the time) have not led to clarifications; many requests were similar to ones raised before them, and the Committee subsequently saw no need to issue additional clarifications.

190. After the 2011 review, the Guidelines clarification procedure, in principle, works as follows (although no new clarifications have either been requested or issued since NCPs obtained their current status in 2000). Before the Committee can be approached with a request for clarification, parties that are uncertain about the Guidelines' applicability in a particular context or want to signal an alleged violation, first need to approach the relevant NCP. Enterprises, business and labour organizations and any other interested party may raise such issues. If an enterprise is directly concerned, the NCP should contact the enterprise to inform it that an issue related to the Guidelines has been raised. The Contact Point, management and labour representatives and other interested parties then try to settle the matter. As noted above, it would be appropriate for the NCP initially addressed to contact other NCPs if the issue under consideration concerns more than one adhering country.

191. Whenever an NCP gives its opinion as to the relevance of the Guidelines in specific instances, it ought to keep in mind the international character of the Guidelines and the need to avoid conflicting national interpretations. To prevent variations in the meaning of Guidelines provisions is an underlying concern of the Investment Committee. It will consider requests from an NCP for assistance where there is any doubt about the interpretation of the Guidelines in particular circumstances. It may also consider a substantiated submission by an adhering government, an advisory body or OECD Watch on whether an NCP has correctly interpreted the Guidelines in a specific instance. The Committee then discuses the matter, consults with stakeholders and may, as a result, issue a clarification of how the Guidelines apply in a situation like the one in question. However, any clarification represents no more and no less than the application of the Guidelines to the issue raised. The clarification is not supposed to be a judgment on the behaviour of an individual enterprise; hence, clarifications that have arisen in connection with individual firms, have never referred to them by name.[55]

192. Thus, final responsibility for guidance and clarification lies with the Committee, although it relies on the NCPs to ensure as far as possible that the meaning of the Guidelines is clear in each national context. It seems only natural that the Committee that drafted the Guidelines and recommends them to MNEs should also, when problems arise in applying them, clarify uncertainties. These uncertainties may not only be due to the fairly general formulation of the Guidelines, which often hides difficult compromises among the countries that negotiated the text, but also to the diversity of the different national systems and practice to which they apply, as well as to the complexity of the problems and factual situations involved. Finally, the fact that since the 2000 Review no cases have come up to the Committee level for clarification seems to substantiate the view that NCPs, as a rule, now work quite efficiently, and that the Committee's involvement in clarifying particular sections or provisions may no longer be needed.

IV. Implementation in Non-adhering Countries

193. The MNE Guidelines request observance of their standards and principles by enterprises wherever they operate, and not only in the OECD area. Hence, the Council Decision and Procedural Guidance also provide for implementation of the Guidelines in non-adhering countries. For instance, NCPs are expected to respond to enquiries from governments of non-adhering countries. In the case of specific instances arising in a non-adhering country, effective implementation of the Guidelines is in fact more difficult, particularly due to the absence of an NCP. Nonetheless, NCPs are encouraged to take steps to develop an understanding of the issues at stake by means of enquiries and fact-finding activities, for instance through contacts with the management of the firm in the home country or with embassies and government officials and other relevant actors in the non-adhering host country. This is all the more important since in recent years a majority of cases – including cases of criminal neglect of Guidelines standards, leading to many casualties – have tended to arise in non-adhering countries

V. The Need for Further Improvement of Implementation Mechanisms

194. The quality and efficiency of NCP operations still vary widely between countries. There have been a number of complaints by stakeholders that certain

55. The Committee and the Council Decision have consistently used the term 'clarification'. By contrast, 'interpretation' is the preferred term at the International Labour Office, when handling cases under its Tripartite Declaration of Principles on Multinational Enterprises and Social Policy. The policy under both procedures of not naming companies is of course often illusory, since the interested public can, in most cases, easily deduct the particular case and issue involved.

NCPs arenot meeting the criteria laid out in the Procedural Guidance; that they have not been given the necessary resources by governments; or that they impose excessively restrictive requirements for their acceptance of specific instances. In some cases NCPs are hardly visible or appear to exist only 'on paper'. For example, in early 2016 seven adhering countries did not have a website in place outlining the NCP mechanism.

195. The OECD Secretariat has developed a strategy to help NCPs improve their performance. To increase NCPs' visibility, it is offering its guidance on good practice for setting up a website and for disseminating useful communications material. To improve transparency and accountability, it also urges all NCPs to provide annual reports to the Secretariat (i.e. to respond to the common reporting framework), and to publish them on their website. As to controversies arising during the handling of specific instances, it invites BIAC, TUAC and OECD Watch to make a formal submission to the Investment Committee, after which the Working Party on Responsible Business Conduct will take appropriate action.

196. Thus, the OECD Secretariat is aiming to help adhering countries comply with their obligations, and NCPs to discharge their functions as required under the OECD Council Decision on implementation. Major tools in this assistance are peer reviews and capacity building missions. Peer reviews are being organized country by country, with the intention to assess the internal workings of an NCP and both good practices and possible deficiencies and barriers that NCPs may face in realizing their objectives. For countries not considered 'peer-review ready', in particular recent adherents, the Secretariat proposes 'capacity-building support' by means of visits to the country, followed up by a report with a set of recommendations.[56]

§4. Positions by TUAC, BIAC and OECD Watch on the Implementation of the Guidelines

197. The Trade Union Advisory Committee is a strong supporter of the Guidelines, has given many inputs to the 2011 update, in particular, and is undertaking important efforts to ensure their implementation. For example, TUAC has organized workshops, both in adhering and non-adhering countries, to raise awareness of the Guidelines. It has developed a manual explaining to trade unions how to use the complaints mechanism[57] and has carried out surveys among its affiliates regarding their experience and involvement with NCPs.

198. Trade unions have raised almost half of all cases brought since the 2000 review. In TUAC's view, the responses from NCPs to the cases raised are often not satisfactory ('the overall performance of NCPs is uneven and in all too many cases

56. See the documents of the Working Party on Responsible Business Conduct, (i) 'Addressing issues relating to the functioning and performance of NCPs;, 10 March 2015 ; and (ii) 'Implementation of an Action Plan to Strengthen National Contact Points', 25 September 2015.
57. TUAC, *The OECD Guidelines for Multinational Enterprises*, Trade Union Guide, Paris 2012

poor'). TUAC notes a lack of 'timely' response as required in the Procedural Guidance, as well as a lack of transparency throughout the procedures, and argues that in too many cases NCPs have refrained in the past from making results publicly available. While the Guidelines now require NCPs to issue a final statement, too many of them still refrain from making a clear statement as to whether activities of a company in question constituted a breach of the Guidelines. On the issue of 'parallel proceedings', trade unions have complained for a long time that certain NCPs use the fact that cases are being treated in legal jurisdictions as an excuse for not dealing with them, and that this practice continues despite the most recent recommendation to the contrary in the Procedural Guidance (see above).

199. Following the 2011 update, the Trade Union Advisory Committee reminded the OECD that the 'success of the update depends on its … full implementation', and that it was of prime importance to 'upgrade the structures and procedures of NCPs', some of which TUAC considered practically 'invisible'.[58] It also developed a checklist for NCPs to determine whether they had brought in line their practices with the Procedural Guidance and published profiles of NCP performance on the TUAC website.[59] As part of its 15-Point Plan of 2015 to make implementation procedures more effective, TUAC requests, *inter alia*, to (a) increase human and financial resources to NCPs; (b) comply with the timeframes set out for the various procedures in the Council's Procedural Guidance and speed up the resolution of cases raised; (c) apply a sufficiently low threshold for the acceptance of cases at the initial assessment phase; and (d) provide for consistent follow-up in NCP final statements or reports to verify over time whether mediation results and NCP recommendations are effectively implemented.[60]

200. High on the TUAC agenda is also the need for regular contacts with the social partners and the need for tripartite or multipartite NCP structures where the trade unions would be involved. TUAC also suggests to fund a roster of mediators for assistance in specific instances, set up a system of 'shadow reporting' by external stakeholders accompanying NCP procedures, and strengthen the programme of peer review both for existing NCPs and for countries wanting to adhere to the Guidelines.

201. The Business and Industry Advisory Committee also endorses the Guidelines text and recommends their observance to its member organizations and all enterprises as being 'in the best interest of business'.[61] It also accepted the substantive 2011 revisions, 'although the new text increases the expectations put on business in a number of aspects'. Indeed, during the negotiations, BIAC support was at

58. TUAC Submission to the OECD Working Group of the Investment Committee, 30 September 2011, http://www.tuac.org (papers on multinationals and trade)
59. http://www.tuacoecdmneguidelines.org/NCPcomparisonAll.asp
60. TUAC, 15-point plan for National Contact Points, http://www.tuacoecdmneguidelines.org/Docs/TUAC-15PointPlan-NCP15.pdf
61. See BIAC's information manual: *Responsible Business Conduct: The OECD Guidelines for Multinational Enterprises*, Paris, June 2015. The business case for CSR and Human Rights due diligence was also developed by a group of employer associations (BDA, MEDEF, Confindustria),

times in doubt, since it argued strongly against (i) replacing the term 'employee' by 'worker' throughout the text and in particular in the Employment and Industrial Relations chapter; and (ii) the burden put on enterprises asked to prevent or mitigate adverse impacts which are caused by their business partners. Reviewing the revised text about due diligence to avoid adverse impact, BIAC stresses the principle that 'MNEs are responsible for their own behaviour and not for the adverse impacts purely caused by others'.[62]

202. BIAC continues to stress the voluntary character of the Guidelines and considers it crucial that they remain part of the OECD Declaration on International Investment and Multinational Enterprises, so that the focus is on a package based on mutual commitment. It also urges the OECD to promote convergence of corporate social responsibility standards between adhering and non-adhering countries in order to create a level playing field in global markets.[63]

203. Concerning the implementation process, BIAC advocates flexible procedures and avoiding 'excessively broad interpretations' of particular Guidelines provisions by NCPs. Based on surveys of member companies' experiences in NCP specific instance procedures, BIAC warns against confrontational, campaign-oriented approaches of complainants, which is considered anathema to impartial solutions found through conciliation and mediation. The start of a specific instance should not be mistaken as the start of a prosecution and does not, of itself, imply any violation on the part of the company. NCPs should avoid taking on cases that coincide with collective bargaining negotiations and should suspend any involvement during the course of parallel legal or administrative proceedings. They should carefully respect confidentiality requirements and not publicize information about specific instances, as long as cases are pending. In case of media campaigns or the spreading of untrue information by a complainant, NCPs should consider early termination of the process. On the other hand, BIAC has published a joint statement with TUAC and OECD Watch, supporting efforts 'to further strengthen the performance of NCPs … including through the exchange of best practices and the organization of peer reviews', and calling on governments to adequately equip and staff their contact points.[64]

204. The views of OECD Watch on the Guidelines' implementation procedures are similar to those of TUAC, and to some extent even more critical. It requests of

---

in partnership with BUSINESSEUROPE, the IOE and the Training Centre of the ILO, A Guide on CSR and Human Rights – what does it mean for companies in supply chains? (https://www.businesseurope.eu/publications/guide-csr-and-human-rights-what-does-it-mean-companies-supply-chains).

62. See the BIAC contribution to the OECD Global Forum on Responsible Business Conduct, 26–27 June, 2014, where BIAC argues, 'it has been claimed by some that a simple business relationship with a supplier would establish responsibility of an MNE for any adverse impact brought about by that supplier in the supply chain of the MNE, regardless of the specifics of the link of the MNE to this impact. We strongly advise against such a broad interpretation …'
63. BIAC Secretariat note on 'The outcome of the updated OECD MNE Guidelines', July 2011.
64. BIAC, OECD Watch, TUAC, Joint Statement October 2015, www.biac.org.

the INV Committee to ensure more rigorously that NCPs are functioning properly, preferably by revising the Procedural Guidance and setting more specific minimum standards for NCP functioning. Its review of 15 years of cases brought before NCPs found that some NCPs set unreasonably high barriers for accessing the complaint mechanism; that they prioritize confidentiality over transparency; do not comply with procedural timelines; and sometimes confusingly interpret the Guidelines provisions in vastly different ways. Their stocktaking culminates in the critical assessment that 'the overwhelming majority of complaints have failed to bring an end to corporate misconduct or provide remedy for past or on-going abuses ...'[65]

65. OECD Watch, *Remedy Remains Rare*, An analysis of 15 years of NCP cases and their contribution to improve access to remedy for victims of corporate misconduct , Amsterdam 2015; see also OECD Watch, *Calling for Corporate Accountability*: a guide to the 2011 0ECD guidelines for multinational Enterprises, June 2013. By contrast, the OECD Secretariat points out that over a third of recent cases have resulted in an internal policy change of the company in question (OECD, Inplementing the OECD Guidelines for Multinational Enterprises: The National Contact Points from 2000 to 2015, Key Findings, Paris 2016).

Concluding Remarks

205. The most recent updates of the OECD Guidelines have substantially strengthened their content and implementation procedures. Among all international CSR instruments, the Guidelines clearly have the strongest implementation mechanism. They now incorporate all core labour standards as set out by the ILO – including freedom-of-association and the right to collective bargaining, the prohibition of child labour and compulsory labour, and non-discrimination – and include new or strengthened provisions concerning, among other things, respect for human rights, the provision of adequate wages and working conditions, labour/management cooperation and reasonable notice prior to final decisions being taken. Terminology relating to 'workers' or 'employees' has been altered so as to make it more difficult to circumvent the Guidelines by recourse to disguised employment relationships. Further, in view of sub-standard conditions in many subcontracting firms in developing countries, MNEs have been given new responsibilities for ensuring the observation of Guidelines standards in their supply chain.

206. Implementation procedures have much improved since the 2000 review, in particular by strengthening the role of the NCPs that all adhering countries are required to establish, even if their effectiveness continues to vary considerably. The number of 'specific instances' raised before NCPs already surpasses many times the number of clarifications sought from the CIME between 1976 and 2000, implying that the relevant actors believe that the Guidelines can be made to work to their mutual advantage.

207. With increasing global economic exchange and multilateral investment, the Guidelines continue to face important challenges. First, the OECD's guidance on NCP implementation procedures needs to fill existing gaps and tackle operational deficiencies. Further, public recognition of the Guidelines as an instrument of corporate social responsibility is far from optimal. Many firms, NGOs and trade unions simply do not know enough about the Guidelines and their complaint procedures. Continuous and increased coordination with other corporate responsibility instruments (ILO, UN, private initiatives) will be helpful to raise awareness of CSR issues. It is particularly important to maintain the consistence between the ILO and OECD instruments.

208. For the Guidelines to succeed as a mediation and problem-solving instrument, NCPs need to ensure that they are perceived as accessible and responsive, and that they respond to specific instances using adequate timeframes. As many cases involve actors from several countries, coordination between the NCPs is essential. In addition, transparency is an ever-present concern. The INV Committee tried to clarify the principles underlying confidentiality and transparency during the negotiations leading up to the 2011 update, but the issue remains contentious between trade union or NGO notifiers of specific instances on the one hand, and the business community, on the other. Results of NCP proceedings should normally be transparent, and attempts to anonymize company names in NCP statements seem unproductive, as they were previously in clarifications by the Investment Committee.

209. Twelve non-OECD countries have adhered to the Guidelines by early 2016 and have set up their respective implementation machinery. However, there are many more emerging and crucial economies that have not adhered, with Brazil, China, India, Russia and Indonesia being some of the more important ones. Without a Contact Point, an important partner in the Guidelines process is missing in these countries. But it is here that the Guidelines' credibility as an instrument for the social monitoring of MNEs' worldwide activities is at stake.

Selected Bibliography

BIAC (Business and Industry Advisory Committee to the OECD), *Responsible Business Conduct: The OECD Guidelines for Multinational Enterprises*, Paris, June 2015.

BIAC, *Contribution to the OECD Global Forum on Responsible Business Conduct,* 26–27 June, 2014.

BIAC, The outcome of the updated OECD MNE Guidelines, Secretariat note, July 2011.

BIAC, OECD Watch, TUAC, *Joint Statement (on OECD Guidelines and National Contact Points)*, October 2015, www.biac.org.

Blanpain, R., *The Badger Case and the OECD Guidelines for Multinational Enterprises*, Deventer, Kluwer, 1977.

Blanpain, R., *The OECD Guidelines for Multinational Enterprises and Labour Relations. 1976–1979, Experience and Review*, Kluwer, 1979; 1979–1982, *Experience and Mid-Term Report*, Kluwer 1983; and *1982–1984, Experience and Review Report*, Kluwer 1985.

Blanpain, R., 'Guidelines for Multinational Enterprises, for Ever? The OECD Guidelines, 20 years later', *International Journal of Comparative Labour Law and Industrial Relations*, 14/4, pp. 337–348, 1998.

European Commission, *Communication from the Commission to the European Parliament, the Council, the European Economic and Social Committee and the Committee of the Regions, A renewed EU strategy 2011-14 for Corporate Social Responsibility*, Brussels, 25.10.2011, COM(2011) 681.

French National Contact Point, *NCP Report on Implementation of the OECD Guidelines in the Textile and Clothing Sector*, December 2013, www.tresor.economic.gouv.fr/File/39881.

Goldman, A.L. and R.L. Corrada, *Labor Law and Industrial Relations in the United States of America* (2010), National Monograph in: *International Encyclopaedia for Labour Law and Industrial Relations*, Kluwer, Netherlands.

ILO, *Tripartite Declaration of Principles concerning Multinational Enterprises and Social Policy*, International Labour Office, Geneva, 4th edn, 2006.

ILO, *The Employment Relationship: An Annotated Guide to ILO Recommendation No. 198,* May 2007, http://www.ilo.org/ifpdial/areas-of-work/labour-law/WCMS_172417/lang–en/index.htm.

International Training Centre of the ILO, in partnership with BUSINESSEUROPE, the IOE, BDA, MEDEF and Confindustria, *A Guide on CSR and Human Rights – what does it mean for companies in supply chains*? Turin, 2015 (https://www.businesseurope.eu/publications/guide-csr-and-human-rights-what-does-it-mean-companies-supply-chains).

Selected Bibliography

OECD, *Review of the 1976 Declaration and Decisions on International Investment and Multinational Enterprises,* Paris 1979.

OECD, *The OECD Guidelines for Multinational Enterprises*, Paris 1986.

OECD, *The OECD Guidelines for Multinational Enterprises*, Paris 1994.

OECD, *OECD Guidelines for Multinational Enterprises. Global Instruments for Corporate Responsibility*, Annual Report 2001, Paris 2001.

OECD, *OECD Guidelines for Multinational Enterprises. Focus on Responsible Supply Chain Management*, Annual Report 2002, Paris 2002.

OECD, *The OECD Guidelines for Multinational Enterprises, A Key Corporate Responsibility Instrument*, Policy Brief, June 2003.

OECD, *OECD Risk Awareness Tool for Multinational Enterprises in Weak Governance Zones*, Paris 2006.

OECD, *Labour and the OECD: the Role of TUAC'*, OECD Policy Brief, December 2008, http://www.tuac.org/en/public/tuac/0812_TuacRole.pdf.

OECD, *Annual Report on the OECD Guidelines for Multinational Enterprises 2008, Employment and Industrial Relations,* Paris 2008.

OECD, *Annual Report on the OECD Guidelines for Multinational Enterprises 2011, A New Agenda for the Future*, Paris 2011.

OECD, *Annual Report on the OECD Guidelines for Multinational Enterprises 2012, Mediation and Consensus Building,* Paris 2012.

OECD, *Annual Report on the OECD Guidelines for Multinational Enterprises 2013, Responsible business conduct in action,* Paris 2013.

OECD, *Annual Report on the OECD Guidelines for Multinational Enterprises 2014, Responsible business conduct by sector,* Paris 2014.

OECD, *Annual Report on the OECD Guidelines for Multinational Enterprises 2015,* Paris 2016.

OECD, *OECD Due Diligence Guidance for Responsible Supply Chains of Minerals from Conflict-affected and High-risk Areas*, 3rd edn, Paris 2016.

OECD, *Implementing the OECD Guidelines for Multinational Enterprises: The National Contact Points from 2000 to 2015,* Key Findings, Paris 2016.

OECD, Database of specific instances, http://mneguidelines.oecd.org/database/

OECD Council, *Recommendation of the Council on Common Approaches for Officially Supported Export Credits and Environmental and Social Due Diligence*, June 2012 (available as OECD document TAD/ECG(2012)5).

OECD and FAO, *OECD–FAO guidance for Responsible Agricultural Supply Chains,* Paris 2016.

OECD Watch, *Calling for Corporate Accountability: A Guide to the 2011 OECD Guidelines for Multinational Enterprises*, June 2013.

OECD Watch, *Quarterly Case Update*, Vol 10, No. 1, June 2015.

OECD Watch, *Remedy Remains Rare: An Analysis of 15 years of NCP Cases and their Contribution to Improving Access to Remedy for Victims of Corporate Misconduct*, Amsterdam 2015.

Rüb, S., *World Works Councils and other Forms of Global Employee Representation in Transnational Undertakings*, Hans Böckler Stiftung, Working Paper 55, Düsseldorf, 2002.

Salzman, J., 'Labor Rights, Globalization and Institutions: The Role and Influence of the Organization for Economic Cooperation and Development', *Michigan Journal of International Law*, Vol. 21, No. 4, 2000.

Tergeist, P. *et al.*, *The Organization for Economic Co-operation and Development, International Encyclopaedia for Labour Law and Industrial Relations*, Vol. 2, supplement 235, October 2000.

Terms of reference of the OECD Investment Committee, http://webnet3.oecd.org/OECDgroups/.

Terms of reference for 2011 update of OECD Guidelines for Multinational Enterprises, http://www.oecd.org/corporate/guidelinesformultinationalenterprises/45124171.pdf.

TUAC (Trade Union Advisory Committee of the OECD), *Trade Union Cases, Key Statistics*, www.tuacoecdmneguidelines.org/statistics.asp.

TUAC Submission to the OECD Working Group of the Investment Committee 30 September 2011, http://www.tuac.org.

TUAC, *The OECD Guidelines for Multinational Enterprises*, Recommendations for Responsible Business Contact in a Global Context, Trade Union Guide, Paris 2012.

TUAC, *15-point Plan for National Contact Points*, http://www.tuacoecdmneguidelines.org/Docs/TUAC-15PointPlan-NCP15.pdf.

UN Human Rights Council, 17th Session, Report of the Special Representative of the Secretary-General on the issue of human rights and transnational corporations and other enterprises, John Ruggie, Guiding Principles on Business and Human Rights, Implementing the United Nations 'Protect, Respect and Remedy' Framework, document A/HRC/17/31, 21 March 2011.

Selected Bibliography

Index

The terms 'multinational enterprises (MNEs) and 'OECD Guidelines for Multinational Enterprises' have not been included in the index, since they come up throughout the text. Further, the index does not refer to additional terms used in the footnotes. Numbers given refer to paragraphs.

Index

Index

Index